THE TAX TICKING TIME BOMB

THE TAX TICKING TIME BOMB

How to Recognize and Manage Tax Traps in Retirement

BILL MULLEN CFP®, MBA

Published in the United States by
Mullennium Publishing.

ISBN: 978-0-9980846-0-2

Book cover design by: Michelle Rayner, Cosmic Design

Interior design by: Katie Mullaly, Faceted Press

This book is dedicated to my wife Carole and our
12 Grandchildren: Andrew, Allie, Katherine, Matthew, Jaden,
McKenna, Ashley, Drew, Jimmy, Josh, Dayton and Kaley.

They are young enough to make the trek up the mountain
and get down safely. All they have to do is practice
what is contained in the following pages.

12/15/16

Ashley,

Happy 21st birthday.
My greatest wish for you is
to take to heart what I
have written in the first
half of this book.

Grandpa

TABLE OF CONTENTS

FOREWORD

Many books on investing and retirement focus on building up funds like 401(k)s, 403(b)s, 457 plans and IRAs so that you can spend your golden years in comfort. Although the early chapters of this book provide you with ways to save, the later chapters deal with the pitfalls of taxes and increased Medicare premium costs during the years you thought were going to be stress free.

And therein lies the conundrum. It seems to me that all books on the financial aspect of retirement focus on savings, but not very many (if at all) show you how to handle your finances when you retire. In other words, how you must plan in retirement to make sure you have all the money you need for as long as you live.

That is where I come in. In fact, it is my main focus in preparing my clients for their retirement.

A good analogy about life regarding your working years and your years in retirement is to compare it to conquering Mount Everest.

- It takes study, preparation and time to get ready to achieve the summit.
- Trying to climb Mount Everest on a shoe string budget is both dangerous and foolhardy.
- Getting to the top is one thing; getting down safely is of the utmost importance.

Each of those points is relevant to you in achieving a successful retirement. For years, the emphasis of planners and thinkers has been to focus on points one and two while ignoring the third point. If you Google "How much does it cost to climb Mount Everest?" you might come across an article written by Ron Haynes who is Certified as a Professional Behavioral, Motivator, and Emotional Intelligence Analyst. That is quite a title. In Mr. Haynes' Google search on the cost of an Everest excursion, he found the answer to be, "...as much as a $100,000." But the more interesting fact that he discovered was that **80 PERCENT OF ALL ACCIDENTS THAT OCCUR WHEN CLIMBING MT. EVEREST HAPPEN ON THE WAY DOWN!**

On July 1, 2016, the first of the baby boomers turned 70½. At age 70½, anyone no longer working and holding tax deferred accounts like those mentioned previously, are subject to the dreaded Required Minimum Distribution (RMD) rules. The operative word is REQUIRED. Put another way, those funds you have worked so hard to build, are not owned by you alone. You have had a silent partner who is now vocal. Uncle Sam wants his reward for allowing you to coast through all those years, tax free. The more you have saved in tax deferred accounts, the more you will owe the IRS. YOU DO NOT HAVE A CHOICE! Come 70½, money must begin to be removed from these type of accounts EACH YEAR whether you need the money or not. And all that money is taxable money.

The old thinking was that it is best to sock away as much money as you can in tax deferred accounts because you will be in a lower tax bracket when you retire. That may be true for some but it may not be true for you. Why? If you saved a big pile of money, maybe bigger than you planned, and now you are forced to withdraw it, this puts you in a big pile of money tax bracket. Trust me, you will not be happy. Not being happy in retirement is not a good plan.

Planning in retirement will be more important than planning was during your climb up the mountain. In this book I show you how to plan for your years in retirement and keep the tax man at bay, so you can enjoy your hard-earned savings.

There is another reason to be concerned about taxes when you retire. The United States has a national debt fast approaching $20,000,000,000,000. That is TWENTY TRILLION DOLLARS; it stands to reason that taxes will be higher in the future rather than be lower. The idea of disbursing your money later in life, when you are supposedly in a lower tax bracket, did not take into account that taxes in those brackets would be much higher at that late date. Recognizing this as a real problem, I have spent time in this book to help you plan ways to keep taxes and Medicare premiums as low as possible in retirement, while still affording you the retirement you want and deserve.

My goal is to help you get safely down the mountain.

WT Mullen
Copyright September 25, 2016

PART ONE
THE SAVING YEARS
The Climb Up the Mountain

CHAPTER 1
Decisions, Decisions

"If you don't know where you are going, any road will get you there."
- Lewis Carroll

DECISION NUMBER ONE

The first decision for an investor is fairly easy. Will you do it yourself or will you hire help? "Hire" is the correct term. Even if you do it yourself you will have to spend some money on books, magazines and time educating yourself. There is no doubt that many people can become successful investors without paying someone else. However, the average person doesn't want to spend the time. If you decide to do it yourself, keep reading because my suggestions are designed to make you successful. If you do it yourself, you will save yourself a lot of time and money *if* you ignore the talking heads on TV that tell you which way the investment markets will go and what stocks to buy. Further, I advise you not to look at the daily, weekly, or monthly returns. Investing is a journey not a 100 yard dash.

DECISION NUMBER TWO

Your second decision is to determine your investment philosophy. You may not even think there is such a thing as an investment philosophy, but there is. In fact, there are two; either you believe the market is efficient or you believe it is not.

If you believe the market is efficient then you buy into this: The market value at any time, i.e. the current price, reflects the supply and demand for any and all stocks. That means you assume the market price reflects all available information about stocks. And only new and unknowable information and events can change the price. In other words, you believe that the markets work.

Having this kind of faith in the market leads to the obvious conclusion that investors cannot beat the market. Although that might appear to be a devastating conclusion, it really is a liberating revelation. Why? Because it liberates you (the investor) from looking for the next big discovery on how to beat the market. This gives you the freedom to work on a *realistic* plan that achieves market returns. Achieving market returns can be very rewarding. For example, in Chapter 2, I show you how far the average mutual fund investor misses out on achieving market returns.

On the other hand, if you believe the market is inefficient, you assume you (or someone you hire) can beat the market. You can certainly point to individuals who have done so in the past. Perhaps you can even illustrate how an overpriced or underpriced stock made money for its investors. However, you will have the impossible task of demonstrating that someone has been successful over the long term using this approach. This is the belief that Markets Fail

In conclusion, here are your options with each of the two philosophies[1].

1. If you believe FREE MARKETS WORK (THAT THEY ARE EFFICIENT), then you:
    - Focus on capturing market returns
    - Utilize asset-class or structured funds

---

1 *Main Street Money, How to Outwit, Outsmart & Out Invest the Wall Street Bullies* , Chapter 3 pages 45-49. Mark Matson, McGriff Video Publications LLC Copyright 2012

    - Diversify prudently
    - Identify your risk tolerance
    - Eliminate traditional investment strategies
    - Work with a financial coach who shares your market belief. Someone who will keep you on track.

2. If you believe FREE MARKETS FAIL (THAT THEY ARE INEFFICIENT), then you:
    - Pursue traditional investment strategies
    - Stay connected to all sources of financial information
    - Read every investment article you can find
    - Work with a financial professional who shares your market belief

Why is Establishing an Investment Philosophy Important?

You cannot believe some aspects of each of the two philosophies and achieve peace of mind in investing. You will drive yourself crazy. If you conclude that markets are inefficient all or most of the time, the stock market may not be the investment vehicle for you. Real Estate may be the way to go. Or building a business, with the end game of selling it at a great profit, may be another option for you. But I believe the stock market is the greatest vehicle available for creating wealth for you with returns that will give you a comfortable retirement. That said, investing is not a get rich quick scheme. As I said earlier, it is a journey, not a 100 yard dash.

Most investors do not realize you can make a choice about the market. Nor do they realize that choosing the wrong belief will adversely affect their ability to grow a portfolio over the long term. Wall Street, all broker dealers, the financial press, and the talking heads on TV count on the fact that your emotions most often control your investment decisions. That's how they make money. There are some in the investment community that do not have the investor's best interest at heart, first and foremost.

Once you conclude that achieving market returns is the road you want to travel, here are your rewards:

- You can concentrate on achieving market returns.
- You do not have to predict the future.
- You do not have to pick stocks.
- You do not have to time the market.
- You do not have to rely on track record investing.

This will put you on the path to peace of mind investing.

There is an academic way to invest; by following a few key rules, you can achieve investment returns that will allow you to be a successful retiree. Of course, you will have to invest a reasonable amount each and every paycheck; a minimum of 10 to 15%. Using an academic approach does not guarantee you will always have positive annual returns. In fact, based on history, in some years, you will have losses. Based on history, the number of positive years is greater than the number of negative years, so you can achieve a reasonable return on your portfolio over time.

Ben Carlson CFA wrote an article for the *American Association of Individual Investors Journal* November, 2015, in which he posed 10 questions to help define an investing philosophy[2];

2 AAII Journal November 2015 *10 Questions to Help Define Your Personal Investment Philosophy* Ben Carson CFA

1. What are your core investment beliefs?
2. Do you understand your philosophy and why do you believe in it?
3. Do you know the potential risks?
4. Does it suit your personality and individual circumstances?
5. Will your philosophy help you follow whatever strategy you implement?
6. What constraints are necessary for turning your philosophy into a portfolio?
7. What will you own and why will you own it?
8. What will cause you to buy or sell?
9. What will cause you to make changes to your portfolio over time?
10. What types of investments or strategies will you avoid?

How you answer these 10 questions will help you determine whether markets are efficient or inefficient. Do this before you invest one dollar and it will save you many hours of worry over the years.

Some Ideas for Those Who Manage Their Own Investments

You always hear that an investment portfolio should be diversified; meaning you should own a combination of stocks, bonds, and cash, at a minimum. By purchasing mutual funds, which are nothing more than a basket of stocks or bonds or a combination of stocks and bonds, you avoid the responsibility of picking individual stocks and/ or bonds. If you make sure the mutual funds you purchase do not own the same stocks and or bonds, you can achieve diversification with less than a dozen funds. For example, by purchasing the Wilshire 5000 Total Market Index, you own a fund that represents all of the U.S. traded stocks, including stocks in the Dow Jones Industrials, all the stocks in the S & P 500, all the technical stocks, and so forth. You could then look for funds that replicate international equity markets, emerging equity markets and then further diversify by adding bond funds. The same approach could be accomplished using Exchange Traded Funds (ETFs) instead of mutual funds. Exchange Traded Funds trade like an individual stock and can prove to be more tax efficient than mutual funds.

Another way you can diversify is by researching individuals who have developed diversification investment programs with a history of success (or at least some back testing that compares favorably with market returns) over extended periods of time. Craig Israelsen is a finance professor at Brigham Young University who developed his "7 Twelve® Portfolio"[3] in 2008. He uses either mutual funds or ETFs to construct his portfolios. The "7" stands for seven different asset classes while the "Twelve" stands for twelve individual mutual funds or ETFs that represents the seven asset classes. Each of the twelve funds carries the same weight in the portfolio, i.e. one twelfth or 8.33% each. Professor Israelsen's system to achieve portfolio diversification has become popular with many *do-it-your-selfers* and some advisors.

We will examine the academic findings of investment models in detail in Chapter 4. But before that, I will review with you two personal areas that frustrate investors, which I'll go over in Chapter 2. In Chapter 3 we will cover individuals and groups that do not work in your best interests.

Focus

Abraham Lincoln is credited with saying "If I had 6 hours to cut down a tree, I would spend 4 hours sharpening the ax." You as an

3 http://www.7twelveportfolio.com/

investor should educate yourself, learning how markets work. A good place for you to start is to answer the 10 questions that Ben Carlson posed in his November 2015 article. The most important decision to make is to decide your investment philosophy. Remember there are only two; markets are efficient or markets are inefficient. That does not mean that markets are always totally efficient, but rather a stock's price, represents at any time, the best estimate of the value of the company.

Finally, if you decide to be a *do-it-your-selfer*, have someone who you respect that you can talk to when your portfolio goes south. Historically, markets go up, but the upward trend is not a smooth slope. There will be weeks, months and years when the market loses money. Those are the times that investors lose faith and make serious mistakes that cause major damage to their long term success.

CHAPTER 2
The Investors' Dilemma[1]

"Worry is a cycle of inefficient thoughts whirling around a center of fear."
- Corrie Ten Boom

The Investor's Dilemma

I'm convinced, after almost 25 years of working with clients to help them with investing and retirement that people give little thought about what it takes to live without a paycheck for 20 to 30 years in retirement. I once met with a prospect who was 59 years old, had saved less than $50,000 and wanted to retire in four years. She explained that she had just received a big promotion and would be making well into six figures for the next four years. I ran some numbers with her input, based on her new savings rate, how much income she wanted in retirement and her life expectancy. The numbers did not work out. The sad part of this story is that she lost her job in two years and never did find one that came close to the salary used in her plan.

What causes folks to put off planning for retirement until retirement is close to arriving? I believe that the diagram on the next page explains a lot. Let's consider each of the ovals, all leading to the conclusion of NOT ENOUGH MONEY.

---

1 The majority of this chapter including the opening graphic is based on Chapter 3 of Mark Matson's book, *Main Street Money, How to Outwit, Outsmart & Out Invest the Wall Street Bullies* McGriff Video Publications LLC Copyright 2012 and the PowerPoint Presentation "Separating Myths from Truths-The Story of Investing" Matson Money Investor Education Series

Investors' Dilemma

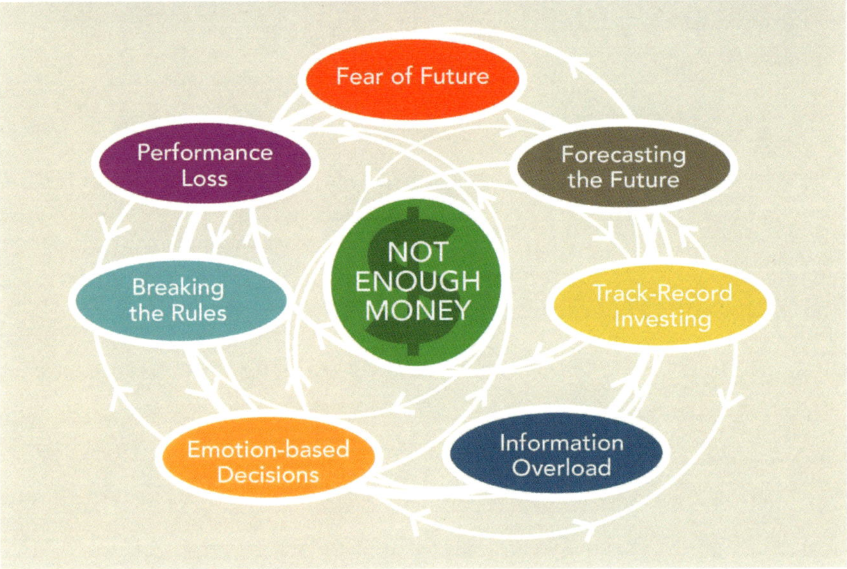

Fear of Future
Performance Loss
Forecasting the Future
NOT ENOUGH MONEY
Breaking the Rules
Track-Record Investing
Emotion-based Decisions
Information Overload

Fear of the Future

For the most part, the only planning many of us do is to plan an annual vacation. Retirement is so far away that it does not require attention when we are in our 20s, 30s, and 40s. When we reach our 50s, a light comes on, but the reality of no paycheck arriving weekly some time down the road is somehow lost in the thought process. It is even more perplexing when some people think that Social Security will not be there when they do retire. That conclusion, which I believe is wrong, starts them thinking. How much will I need in retirement? How much do I need to save? Where should I put my savings? Combine those questions with the messages coming out of the nightly news, the Internet and the remaining newspapers about all the troubles in the world and many give up on the planning process. They just ignore everything and hope it will somehow all work out.

Forecasting the Future

There is often a belief that in order to invest wisely, you need a prediction of what is going to happen in the future. If we just know what is going to occur for the rest of this year and next, *then I will be able to invest wisely.* Nothing is further from the truth. In fact, if your portfolio needs a forecast of the future to be successful, it is already broken. To be a successful investor, predicting the future is not necessary. In fact, trying to predict the future is futile. I admit that there are a number of investment gurus on Wall Street and elsewhere who make a living convincing would-be-investors which stock to buy, which country will beat all others this year, and which companies will be the next Apple, Microsoft, and/or Facebook. The guru makes money selling their advice while the investor loses money. The guru stays in business, because every once in a while the guru is correct and he or she advertises that correct guesstimate to the hilt. I will talk more about gurus in Chapter 3.

Track Record Investing

Will Rogers said that history may not repeat, but it does rhyme. Track Record Investing is the practice of investing in mutual funds because they did well last year or for the last 3 years or because Morningstar awarded it five stars. It is ironic that would-be investors fall for the fallacy of track record investing when the one warning that every prospectus must contain is some variation of the following statement; PAST PERFORMANCE IS NO GUARANTEE OF FUTURE RESULTS. It appears on the prospectus of all 5-star mutual funds as well as all 1-star mutual funds.

Information Overload

If you Google "mutual fund" you will get 38,400,000 results in less than one second. In a quest for peace of mind, investors are forever in search of answers to the question of where and how to invest. They search books, newspapers, magazines, financial talk shows, and the internet. Some even worry when they can't access the internet. I can tell you that for whatever search you follow to reinforce your belief of the moment, you will find it. Here is the truth. If you were to search for the opposite finding, it will be there too.

Emotional Based Decisions

Your brother-in-law, Harry, just made a killing on a stock he heard about, bought it for $10 and it closed yesterday at $22. He called to give you the news and said it was going to $76. Harry is an okay guy and the dopamine flows as you listen to him brag and tell you to jump on this can't-miss chance to make a killing.

Or you just looked at your portfolio and it has been chugging along quite well. For the last three years it has returned 9.2% annually after all fees BUT the 6 o'clock news has been bleak for the last month and it gets worse every night. The market crash is going to be so big that what happened in 2008 is going to look like a little bump in the road.

Here is the truth. Emotions are your worst enemy when it comes to investing. I will discuss emotions and their impact on investing in detail later in Chapter 8. First let me briefly illustrate how emotions lead you to break the Golden Rule of Investing.

Breaking the Rules

Every endeavor has rules and the Golden Rule for successful investing is simple.

- Own Equities long term
- Diversify Globally
- Rebalance

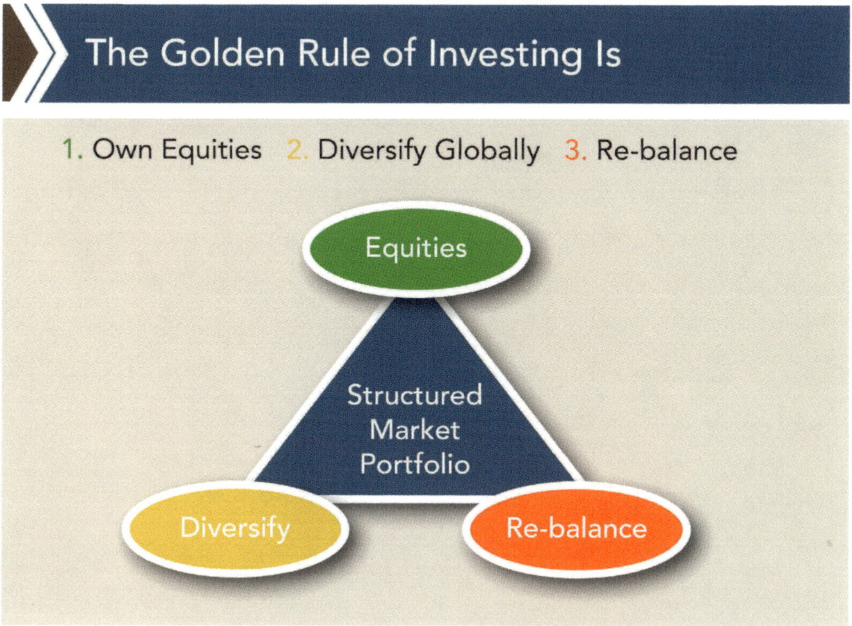

The Golden Rule of Investing Is

1. Own Equities 2. Diversify Globally 3. Re-balance

Equities

Structured Market Portfolio

Diversify

Re-balance

You have to admit the Golden Rule of Investing looks simple. It is simple; unfortunately it is not an easy rule to follow. Here is an example.

You get your statement at the end of 2008. You allocated the portfolio to have 50% in small cap equities and 50% in fixed income-bonds. You are devastated and confused. The long term government bond fund was gang busters returning 25.80%. But the U.S. Small Stock Fund lost 38.67%. Bonds are supposed to be safe and not have big returns. That is what equities are supposed to do.

The bond fund return gives you pleasure and the small cap fund return gives you pain. We humans gravitate toward pleasure and flee from pain. You decide to move all the money that is in the small cap fund and put into the bond fund.

So what happened in 2009? You open your statement at the end of 2009. Here is what you find. The bond fund lost 14.90% and the U.S. Small Cap gained 47.54%. But you did not own any equities.

Instead of rebalancing back to your original targets of 50% bonds and 50% stocks, at the end of 2008, you sold all your stocks and put it all in bonds. You no longer own equities. You no longer are diversified. You have violated all three parts of the Golden Rule. Emotions controlled your decisions. I want you to understand that emotions are the major factors that cause investors to fail!

Performance Loss

It is rare that the average investor achieves the same returns that they see published in the financial section of their local paper or the returns they hear mentioned by the talking heads on television.

Dalbar is a leading financial services research firm located in Boston, Massachusetts. They have been publishing a report since 1994, which shows how the S&P 500 performed over various 20-year periods versus how the average investor has performed over the same period by investing in equity mutual funds. The average investor is defined as someone who has $100,000 invested. The report is referred to as the Quantitative Analysis of Investor Behavior (QAIB). In 2014, Dalbar had 30 years of data. Here is the summary of the Dalbar findings for the thirty years from January 1, 1985 through December 31, 2014.[2]

2 Dalbar 1985-2014 data from Dalbar 303 Congress Street Boston MA 02210

The Average Investor Hardley Earns Enough To Beat Inflation

CATEGORY	1985-2014 Annualized Return
S&P 500 Index	11.16%
Dalbar Average Investor - Equity Fund	3.79%
CPI (representing Inflation)	2.70%

You can see that the difference between what the S&P 500 Index returned (11.16%) and what the average investor returned (3.79%). That is a whopping difference of 7.36 percentage points. **Over 30 years, $100,000 invested at 7.36% would be worth $840,000.**

It should be noted that one cannot invest directly in an index, but one can invest in a surrogate of an index.

All the previous Dalbar reports showed the same kind of differences over the reported 20 year periods as this one shows over this 30 year period. The S&P 500 always out-performs the Dalbar Average Investor-Equity Fund by a substantial margin. But why?

The index covers all 30 years. The average investor is in the market between three to four years over all the studies. The investors get out of the market when markets fall and their emotions take over. You cannot be a successful investor when you let your emotions rule your decisions.

Here is another chart that helps explain investor behavior.[3]

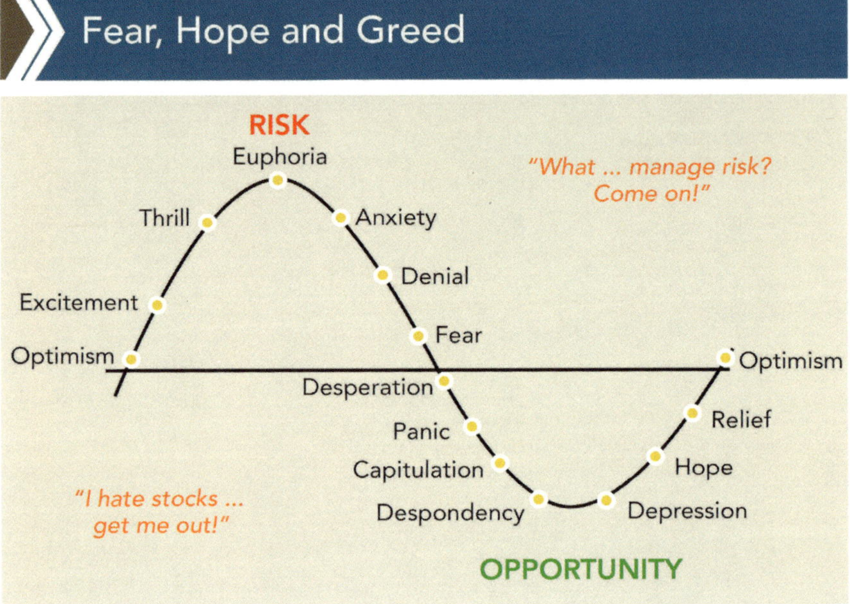

Source: Raymond James Research

There are a couple of subtle lessons that the chart reveals. First, note that the shape of the curve above the horizontal line is higher and wider than the curve below the horizontal line. The market has more up years than down years. Historically, the average market returns over time have been positive. That is also shown by both the S&P 500 index and the average equity investor in the Dalbar table above. Second, note the words associated at the various points along the curve, both above the horizontal and below the horizontal. They all relate to emotions and I have emphasized more than once, emotions are not a friend to you as an investor.

Another issue about returns in any one year is that the expected return of any portfolio will seldom, if ever, achieve that exact number. For

3 Fear, Hope and Greed graph by Raymond James Research

example, if the expected return of your portfolio is an average of 8%, you may never see a year where the return is exactly 8%. The overall average over 20-30 years may be exactly 8% but it is more than likely that not one of the 20-30 years will be 8% or even within ½ of 1% of that number. Here is a graph that illustrates the point.[4]

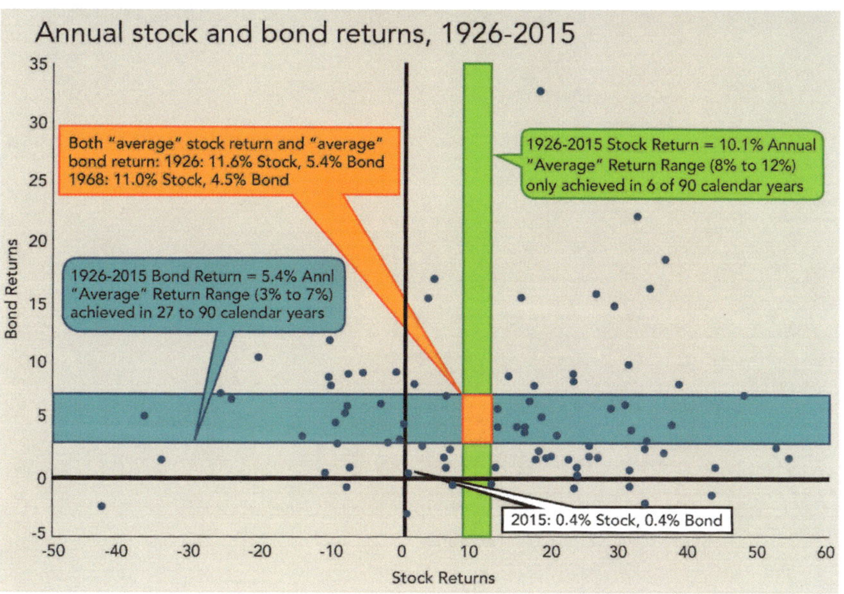

Represents each calendar year from 1926-2015 (90 points = 90 years) plotted at the intersection of that year's stock return and that year's bond return. The vertical shaded area contains all years whose stock return was between 8% and 12%. The horizontal shaded area contains all years whose bond return was between 3% and 7%. Stock return are represented by S&P 90 from 1926 to 3/3/1957, the S&P 500 Index from 3/4/1957 to 1974, the Wilshire 5000 Index from 1975 through April 22, 2005, the MSCI US Broad Market Index from April 23, 2005 until June 2, 2013 and the CRSP US Total Market Index thereafter. Bond returns are represented by S&P High Grade Corporate Index from 1926 to 1968, Citigroup High Grade Index from 1969 to 1972, Lehman Brothers U.S. Long Credit AA Index from 1973 to 1975, the Barclays U.S. Aggregate Bond Index from 1976 through 2009 and the Barclays U.S. Aggregate Float Adjusted Bond Index thereafter. © The Vanguard Group, Inc., used with permission.

4 Vanguard Financial Advisor

Note that in this graph, the average annualized stock return over the period of 1926 through 2014, a period of 89 years, was 10.2% (upper right hand section of the graph). In only 6 of those 89 years did the return fall between 8% and 12%.

Also look at the number of years on the graph where stocks actually lost money. There are 9 years represented by the nine dots that fall below the 0% return line across the bottom of the graph. In addition, there were another 20 plus years that had a return of less than 4%.

Investing is not a smooth ride but you can be a successful investor if you follow the Golden Rule of investing and keep control of your emotions.

The Results

The seven dilemmas addressed in this chapter, cause investors to fear investing, in many cases ending up with not enough money and without peace of mind. Not only are they not where they want to be financially, they have spent a large portion of their lives fraught with stress, anxiety, concern and fear that initiate and perpetuate the Investor's Dilemma.

The good news is there is a way to invest and achieve peace of mind. In Chapter 4, I will lay out the plan. Here is what has happened to long term investors who stayed in the market regardless of what happened yesterday, last week, last month, last year and the years before.[5]

5 http://www.businessinsider.com/charts-that-explain-stock-market-2016-2

Stock Market Since 1900

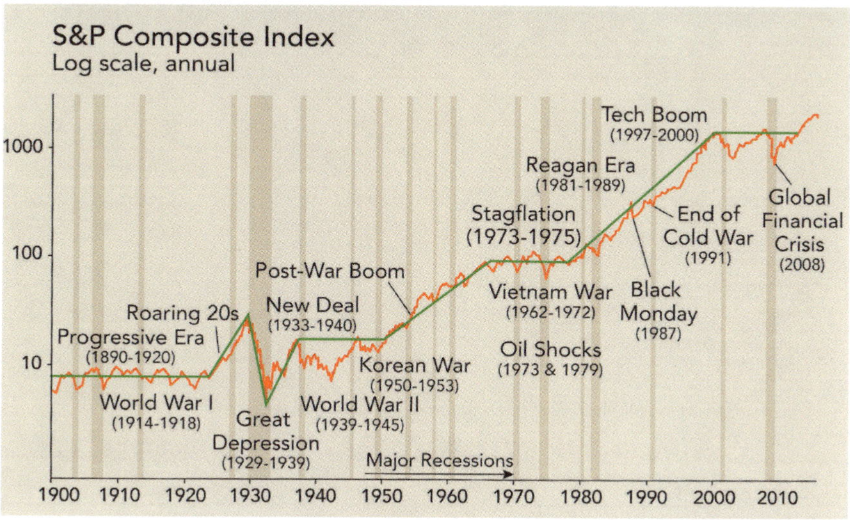

Source: FactSet, NBER, Robert Shiller, J.P. Morgan Asset Management.
Data shown in log scale to best illustrate long-term index patterns.

Look at all the horrible events listed on this graph; two world wars, the Korean and Vietnam Wars, the Great Depression, Black Monday and the real estate crash of 2008. There is always something going on that will pull on you to make a bad decision.

To achieve the long term gains, you must tolerate the short term dips. And yes, I know, past performance is no guarantee of future results.

Focus

I do not want you to ever forget that emotions are enemy number one against your being a successful investor. There are a few groups that know that appealing to your emotions will help them make money, but in the short and long term, cause you to lose money. I will introduce them to you in the next chapter.

CHAPTER 3

Con Men, Prognosticators and Gurus; Plus the Goal of Wall Street

"We are using the word 'guru' only because 'charlatan' is too long to fit into a headline."
- Peter F Drucker

There is another problem for you other than recognizing how emotions can ruin your investing experience that we covered in Chapter 2. That is a group of Wall Street "Experts" who are out for their own self-interest.

Wall Street, the 24-hour financial news, Jim Cramer, and the advice you get from your brother-in-law are all detrimental to your financial well-being. Why? Because these folks (except for maybe your brother-in-law) are in business to make money for themselves, their sponsors, or their companies, but not for you…**definitely not for you!** How do they do that?

- By getting you upset or excited.
- By scaring you or hyping your hopes and dreams.
- By appealing to your emotions, hoping to get you to do something to your portfolio that will not be good for your long term investment health.

They tend to fall into one of three categories; Con Men, Prognosticators, and Gurus. Let's take a look at all three.

Con Men

Most people understand what a con man is, however they also come in the feminine flavor (con woman). The technique under which they work is most often referred to as a Ponzi scheme.[1] It was named after Charles Ponzi, a business man in the 1920s who worked out of his office in Boston, Massachusetts. This type of scam rewards first the con man, then some of the early *investors,* but then fleeces the late comers. A business will often start off as legitimate, but then falls on bad times, because the returns promised on investments do not materialize. A con man who promises higher returns with lower (or no) risk should raise a red flag with you. The early "investors" are paid off as promised and word spreads as to how they have hit pay dirt. The fraud can continue as long as more and more money comes in from new *investors.*

In the 21st century the most famous con man (so far) has been Bernie Madoff.[2] His Ponzi scheme lasted for a very long time. In fact, Madoff's offices were audited no less than eight times over a 16-year period by the U.S. Securities and Exchange Commission (SEC) and other regulatory authorities.[3]

Madoff scammed $50 billion dollars before he was finally caught. Many people lost their life savings. Celebrities such as Elie Wiesel, Larry King, Kevin Bacon, and Jeffrey Katzenberg lost millions of dollars.[4] He is now serving a sentence of 150 years in a federal prison.

---

1 https://en.wikipedia.org/wiki/Charles_Ponzi

2 *Scannell, Kara (January 5, 2009). "Madoff Chasers Dug for Years, to No Avail". The Wall Street Journal. Retrieved January 5, 2009.*

3 ibid

4 http://finance.yahoo.com/news/10-celebrities-scammed-madoff-070142970.html

How do you avoid being scammed? First, if a specific return is promised, that's a red flag. If a return is higher than can be found any place else, that's another red flag. Three of the brightest red flags in the Madoff fraud was he was a) the money manager, b) the custodian of the money, and c) custodian of the firm who issued all statements.

Prognosticators

The next financial experts are the prognosticators. Prognosticators forecast what is going to happen in the future, like fortune tellers. Harry Dent, Jr., represents the modern-day prognosticator. Harry predicted in the late 90s, that the Dow would reach 35,000 or even 40,000 in his book, *The Roaring 2000s: Building the Wealth and Lifestyle You Desire in the Greatest Boom in History*" (1998 Simon & Schuster). So what actually happened from 2000 to 2009 to the S&P 500, which measures the largest 500 stocks in the United States? They had a total return for those ten years of MINUS 9.3% gaining the name for the decade as The Lost Decade.[5]

According to an article in Barons, there were over 300,000 hard cover and paperback copies of The Roaring Twenties sold.[6]

5 http://usatoday30.usatoday.com/money/markets/2010-01-03-2010-outlook-stocks_N.htm

6 http://www.barrons.com/articles/SB899436198468124000

A Lost Decade

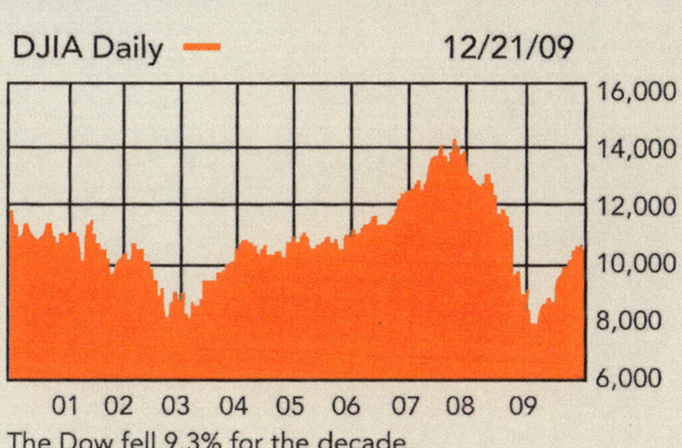

The Dow fell 9.3% for the decade.

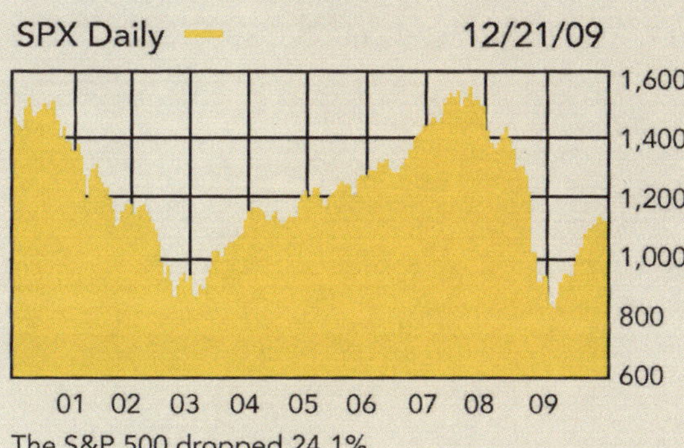

The S&P 500 dropped 24.1%.

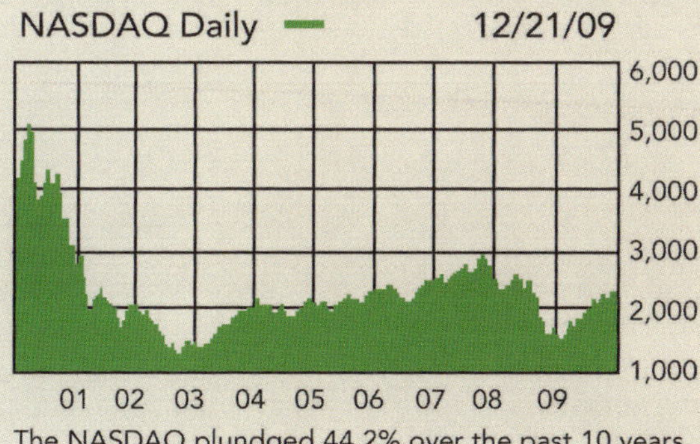

The NASDAQ plundged 44.2% over the past 10 years.

With permission © *Big Charts*

Did missing his forecast by about 70% bother Mr. Dent? Absolutely not! In 2012 he wrote *The Great Crash Ahead: Strategies for a World Turned Upside Down*, (Paperback, September 11, 2012 Free Press a division of Simon & Schuster).

And in 2015 he wrote *The Demographic Cliff: How to Survive and Prosper During the Great Deflation Ahead, (*Paperback, August 25, 2015 Penguin Random House).

His latest forecast is that Stocks will fall by 71% by 2017. You can sign up on-line for the webinar.[7]

Not Even Harry

Harry Dent, Jr., is not the only prognosticator on Wall Street. There are hundreds. They sell lots of books and newsletters. They are guests on financial TV shows, speak at financial conferences, and are never, or hardly ever, called on the carpet for the forecasts they make that never come to pass.

---

7 https://research.economyandmarkets.com/X195S636?gclid=CPbkx_Hk_c4CFZGLaQodkmgEiw

Another prognosticator who constantly forecasts doom and gloom is Porter Stansbury. I will not bore you with Porter's approach, other than to say, he writes newsletters as opposed to books. If you really need more unnecessary doom and gloom in your life, go to this link http://stansberryresearch.com/products/stansberry-s-investment-advisory/.

How do prognosticators survive? Every once in a while one of their forecasts turns out to be true. Think about it. Make enough forecasts over time and one of them will be correct. Then the headline becomes, *Porter was Prescient When He Predicted the (fill in the blank).*

Forecasting the future is gambling and speculating with your money. Is that how you want to save for your future?

All you need to know about the future is that NOBODY CAN KNOW WITH CERTAINTY WHAT IS GOING TO HAPPEN.

The Wall Street Guru

Ken Heebner represents the Wall Street Guru. The Guru is a person who picks individual stocks and times the markets. Many mutual fund managers meet this description, but Ken takes it to extremes. Heebner is the manager of the Capital Growth Manager Focus fund (CGMFX) since 1997. When I looked at CGMFX in the middle of May, 2016, the fund held 20 stocks. According to Yahoo Finance[8], its top 5 holdings represent 75% of the 20 holdings. One of the more revealing facts about the fund is that its turnover ratio is 268%. Think about turnover ratio this way; to have a turnover ratio of 100% means that all the stocks you owned in a fund on Jan 1 would be replaced with totally new stocks by Dec 31. To have

8 http://finance.yahoo.com/q?s=CGMFX

a turnover ratio of 268% means that Heebner is selling the entire portfolio and buying new stocks every 120 days. Remember, that every time there is a sale, there is a cost. Every time there is a buy, there is a cost.

Think about how Heebner manages this fund. First, he picks at least 20 stocks, believing those stocks are going to go up in the short term. Otherwise why would he buy them? Sometime within the next few weeks or months, he will sell them. In the meantime, he buys more stocks with the same thought process in mind. Does any of this make sense? He has been doing this since 1997.

According to a summary about the fund on Yahoo Finance[9] "...the fund typically invests in stocks of between 20 to100 companies at one time...and is flexibly managed so that it can invest in equity securities in a variety of industries as well as in foreign companies. The fund may invest in companies of any size, but primarily invests in companies with market capitalizations of more than $5 billion-large cap companies. If market conditions so warrant, it may establish short positions in specific securities or stock indices. A short position is when you borrow stock and sell it believing that the stock price will fall in the future. If the stock does fall in price, you buy it and return the stock you borrowed. Aside from trying to predict the future by establishing a short position, the fund is non-diversified."

In other words an investor has to put all their faith in Ken Heebner to put their money in the Capital Growth Manager Focus fund. In effect, Heebner is saying to you: TRUST ME.

---

9 http://finance.yahoo.com/q/pr?s=CGMFX+Profile

Like the prognosticators, there are plenty of gurus on Wall Street. If you want to be a successful investor, avoid them. Stock picking and trying to time the market is gambling and speculating with your money.

Understanding the Focus of Wall Street

Wall Street has tens of thousands of people who work with investors. The great majority of them are honest and work to help their clients. There will always be con men, prognosticators and gurus. The latter two think they help investors, but I have my doubts. It is obvious that the con man is out to scam everyone.

You need to be aware that people in the investment industry are in business to make money. There is nothing wrong with making money. Do not think that mutual funds, insurance companies, stock brokers, financial planners, and financial advisors have the same goal as you as an investor.

There are two standards in the financial industry with respect to investing. One is called the **Suitability Standard** and the other is the **Fiduciary Standard**.

- Under the Suitability Standard a stockbroker can sell any product that is suitable to a client. It may not be the best product but as long as it is suitable, the broker is within his or her rights.
- The Fiduciary Standard, on the other hand, demands that the interest of the client's come first and foremost.

As an investor, you should always ask under which standard your advisor operates. In addition, you should ask the following key questions:

1. How is your investment advisor paid?
2. If a product sells is there a commission involved?
3. What are the total commissions paid?
4. How much of any commission goes to your advisor?
5. Are there any penalties in transferring my accounts to your firm?

Focus

Not everyone in the investing community has your best interest in mind. They are in business to make money and the great majority in my mind, are honest. There are some who are not honest and the worst of the dishonest are called Con Men.

That does not mean everyone puts your interest above theirs. Just as I advised you in Chapter 1 to ask a lot of questions before you invest one dollar, ask everyone you deal with how they are paid and how much they are paid. Ask if they are operating under the "Suitability Standard" or if they are using the "Fiduciary Standard" the model in which they are required by law to put your interest FIRST. AFTER ALL, IT IS YOUR MONEY.

Now we are going to look at a method of investing based on decades of academic research, as well as how to remove fear and greed from the investing equation.

CHAPTER 4
The Academic Approach to Investing

"Everyone is entitled to his own opinion, but not his own facts."
- Daniel Patrick Moynihan

Efficient Market Hypothesis

People believe in efficient markets because academicians study stock markets, and provide statistical data that supports the fact that an individual or some entity CANNOT consistently beat the market. But let's face it, even the casual observer can see that markets go up and down. Therefore, it stands to reason that for someone to beat the market all they would have to know is when the market is going to rise and when it is going to fall. That person would just have to buy when the market is going up and sell when it reaches its peak. How hard can that be?

Impossible based on academic studies. Here are a couple of references to academics to consider before buying into the fact that *anyone* can predict the direction of the market:

1. Burton Malkiel's book "*A Random Walk Down Wall Street,*" (W.W. Norton and Company) was first published in 1973 and is now in its 9th edition. All nine editions conclude that a blindfolded chimpanzee, throwing darts at the Wall Street Journal, can select a portfolio that performs as well as those managed by experts. Note the word "blindfolded." There is

no mention of the cost of hiring a chimpanzee versus the fees you pay an expert.

2. Eugene Fama of the University Of Chicago Graduate School Of Business first explained the Efficient Market Hypothesis in his doctoral thesis in 1965 and had this to say: "An efficient market is defined as a market where there are large numbers of rational, profit-maximizers, actively competing with each other, trying to predict future market values of individual securities and where important current information is almost freely available to all participants. In an efficient market, competition among the many intelligent participants leads to a situation where, at any point in time, actual prices of individual securities already reflect the effects of information based both on events that have already occurred and on events which, as of now, the market expects to take place in the future. In other words, in an efficient market, at any point in time, the actual price of a security will be a good estimate of its intrinsic value."[1]

Fama was awarded the Nobel Prize in Economics in 2013 for his work in this area.

Modern Portfolio Theory

Harry Markowitz won the Nobel Prize in Economics in 1990 for his hypothesis that there exists a portfolio which maximizes return for a specified amount of risk. Here is the graph showing Markowitz' findings:

1 Eugene F. Fama, "Random Walks in Stock Market Prices," Financial Analysts Journal, September/October 1965.

Markowitz's Efficient Frontier

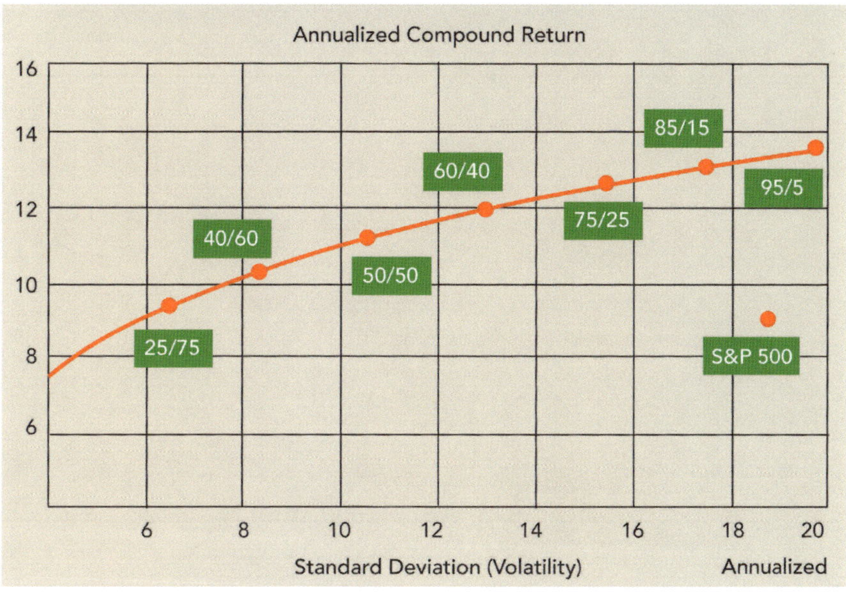

Past Performance is not indicative of future performance. Chart is for illustrative purposes only.

Markowitz plotted the expected return of a portfolio on the Y Axis (vertical) and the risk associated with that portfolio plotted on the X Axis (horizontal). He called the slope of the curve, the Efficient Frontier. Any portfolio below the curve is not efficient. That is because there exists a portfolio that would be directly above and on the Efficient Frontier, thereby providing a higher return for the same amount of risk. Markowitz also stated that no portfolios exist above the Efficient Frontier. The numbers in the green boxes associated with the green dots are the allocation of the various portfolios. The portfolio 25/75 contains 25% equities (stocks) and 75% fixed income (bonds). The 60/40 is a portfolio of 60% equities and 40% bonds, and so on.[2]

2 https://en.wikipedia.org/wiki/Modern_portfolio_theory

The graph also demonstrates that the more fixed income, that is, short term treasury bonds, notes, bills and cash, that a portfolio contains, the less risk in the portfolio.

Notice where the return of the S&P 500 falls in relation to the Efficient Frontier and its associated risk. It is clear that investing in just the S&P 500 gives an annualized return of about 9% with a risk of 19 as measured by standard deviation. Based on Markowitz' research, an investor could achieve a return of about 13% and take the same amount of risk by constructing a portfolio of 90% equity and 10% fixed income which lies on the efficient portfolio directly above where the S&P 500 lies on the graph.

One further point you need to understand. When I talk about achieving market returns, I am not talking about accepting the return of an index such as the market return of the S&P 500 or the Dow Jones Industrial Average. I am talking about constructing a portfolio that lies on the Efficient Frontier; MAXIMUM RETURN FOR THE AMOUNT OF RISK YOU ARE WILLING TO ACCEPT.

A Discussion of Risk

Many investors think of risk as losing all their money in the stock market. I want you to understand how off the wall that thought is. Suppose you invested just in an index that followed the S&P 500. To lose all your money, all 500 of the largest companies in the United States would have to fail. How likely is that? NOT LIKELY AT ALL. Remember, that for you to be a successful investor, you must follow the Golden Rule (Chapter 2) of successful investing, namely;

1. Own Equities
2. Diversify Globally
3. Rebalance

If you do that, you can pretty much forget about losing all your money in the market!

Now that you know that risk does not mean losing all your money in the market, let's look at how I define risk in your portfolio. In the financial world, risk is measured in mathematical terms and is called **standard deviation**. All you need to know about standard deviation is this: the higher the standard deviation, the more your portfolio will have higher ups and lower lows over periods of time. This is referred to as **volatility**. Investors love volatility on the upside, but loathe it on the down side. Actually down side volatility can be the investor's friend. Recall that one of the three parts of the Golden Rule (Chapter 2) of investing is to rebalance the portfolio.

For example, suppose you have a 60/40 portfolio and after a years' worth of ups and downs in the market, the allocation ended at 66/34. That is 66% equities and 34% fixed; more equities and less fixed income. What do you do? You sell equities and buy bonds to get you back to 60/40. For many that may seem counter intuitive. You sold the winner (stocks) and bought the loser (bonds). But think about why that is the right move to make. First, you chose the 60/40 allocation because it provided the return with which you were comfortable based on the risk associated with that portfolio. Second, to leave the allocation at 66/34 means greater volatility than a 60/40 portfolio. You chose a 60/40 mix because that is all the volatility with which you were comfortable. Third, by selling the winner and buying the loser, you have sold high and bought low. That is a winning combination. If you look back at the Dalbar table and the ***Fear, Hope and Greed Chart,*** you see that investors, who fail, buy when the market is high and sell when the market is low. You cannot succeed as an investor by buying high and selling low.

One final point on the use of short term treasury bonds, notes, bills and cash in a portfolio to reduce volatility. It is important for you to understand that **long term bonds in a portfolio will produce more volatility not less.** Why? Because the further into the future that a bond matures, meaning the date it pays back the bond face value, the more it is susceptible to large changes in interest rates. Another way for you to think about it; bonds with a maturity of 10 years or more will have volatility more in line with stocks than with short term treasury bonds, notes, bills and cash.

More on Eugene Fama

As previously mentioned, Eugene Fama won the Nobel Prize in economics in 2013 for his work on efficient markets. In addition, he and Kenneth French from Dartmouth developed The Three Factor Model[3]. Basically it says;

- Equities are riskier than bonds.
- Small cap stocks are riskier than large cap stocks.
- Value stocks are riskier than growth stocks.

As a result of being riskier, equities, small caps, and value stocks create a "risk premium" meaning that by investing in these three categories, investors receive a higher return than they would by investing in bonds, large cap stocks and/or growth stocks.

3 https://portfoliosolutions.com/latest-learnings/fama-french-three-factor-model

Small Stocks & Value Stocks Increase the Expected Return

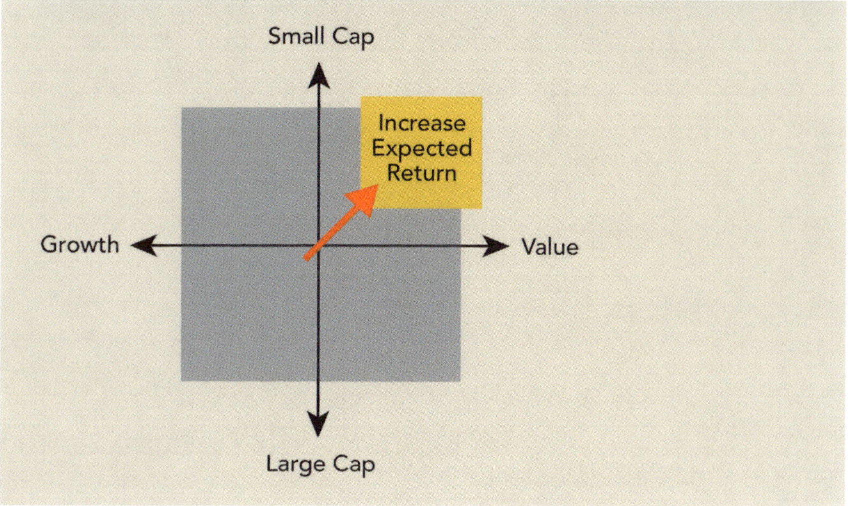

Just to make sure we're all on the same page, a few definitions are in order before we move on:

- Equities, also known as stocks, give the holder of stocks an ownership in a company.
- An owner of bonds means that the bond owner has lent money to a company.
- The word "cap" when associated with a stock refers to the size of a company. Cap is short for capitalization. Cap is equal to the price of one share of stock times the number of shares outstanding. Examples of large cap stocks are Ford Motor Company, Apple, and Google. Examples of small cap stocks are "Children's Place," "Rouse Properties" and "Nautilus." You may have never heard of any of these small cap stocks, but they can still be traded.

Value stocks are stocks of companies that are out of favor with the investment community. The book value of the company is greater than the cap value of the company. In other words the stock sells for less than the net value of the company. Different segments of the market may be out of favor at any one time. For example, when the auto companies were going through the down turn in 2008, all the stocks of the car companies fell. The same thing happened to investment bank stocks during this time frame. It wasn't that these companies were going to fail; they were going through tough times.

Growth stocks are those companies whose recent performance has been good and the future looks positive. Investors believe that these companies will continue to grow. Morningstar is a company located in Chicago.[4] They are one of the biggest, if not the biggest financial company that follows stocks and mutual funds. Initially, Morningstar created the "Style Box," classifying mutual funds into one of nine categories. The classification shown on the next page would be for a mutual fund holding stocks that were large cap and a mixture of both large cap growth and large cap value stocks.[5] It is classified as a "blended fund." An example of a large cap blended fund would be the S&P 500, representing the 500 largest stocks in the United States. The Exchange Traded Fund (ETF) "SPY" is a fund that tracks the S&P 500. Its style box would be the same as the graphic.

---

4. http://www.morningstar.com

5 ©[2016] Morningstar, Inc. All Rights Reserved. The information contained herein: (1) is proprietary to Morningstar and/or its content providers; (2) may not be copied or distributed; (3) does not constitute investment advice offered by Morningstar; and (4) is not warranted to be accurate, complete or timely. Neither Morningstar nor its content providers are responsible for any damages or losses arising from any use of this information. Past performance is no guarantee of future results. Use of information from Morningstar does not necessarily constitute agreement by Morningstar, Inc. of any investment philosophy or strategy presented in this publication.

Morningstar Style Box For Large Cap Blend

By Morningstar's definition, blend represents mutual funds that contain a majority percentage of growth and value stocks. They further differentiate by categorizing by size of the companies in the fund. Medium can be thought of as those companies that have a capitalization that is between large cap and small cap. All these capitalization designations can be broken down further so that there are classifications such as micro caps and mega caps.

The style box was established by Morningstar in 1992. It became apparent over time that having any mutual fund fit nicely into one of those nine boxes was not practical let along realistic. In 2006 the Ownership Zone was created. From the graphic on the next page, you can still see the style box but the designations have been expanded. Instead of having the 3 by 3 matrix, Morningstar expanded to a 5 by 5 matrix. The style box is still used but for an investor who wants to see how diverse the holdings are in any fund, Ownership Zone is a better tool. Think of it as a view from 30,000 feet (style box) versus a view from 100 feet (Ownership Zone).

The Ownership Zone[6] for "SPY" which tracks the S&P 500, is shown in the graphic below.

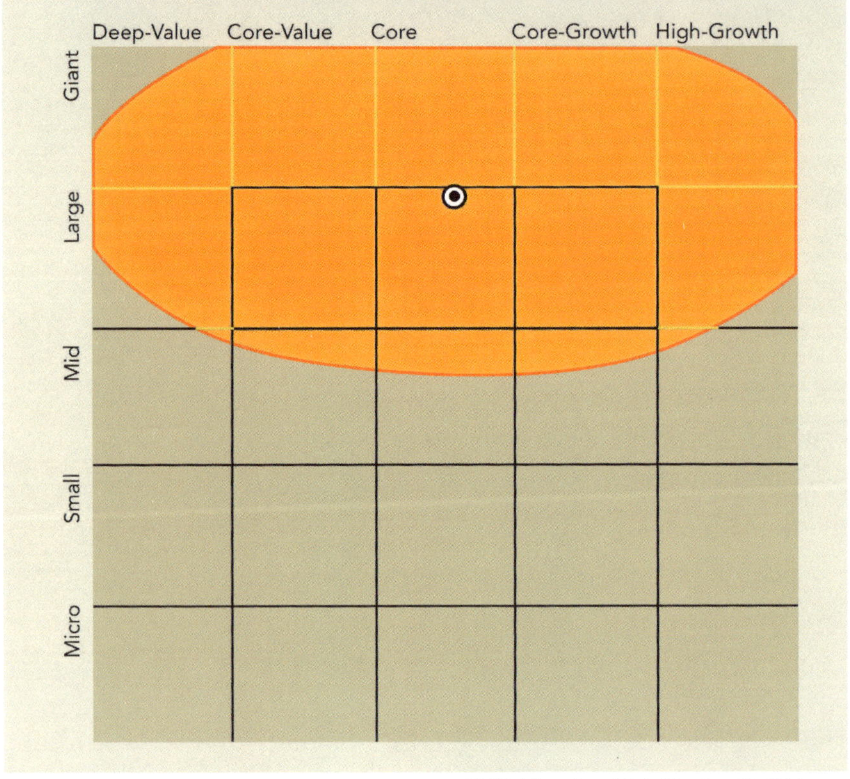

SPY Holdings-Based Style Map Sept 30, 2016

The Center for Research in Security Prices (CRSP) at the University of Chicago divides all the publicly traded stocks in the United States into deciles based on capitalization. The largest companies are in decile 1 and the smallest are in decile 10. Or put another way, mega cap companies are in decile 1 and micro caps are in decile 10[7].

6 ibid

7 http://www.crsp.com/

Academics on Emotions and Investing

In recent years, behavioral economics has become of great interest to many who study investing. In 2002, Daniel Khaneman won the Nobel Prize in Economics for his work in this area[8]. It was the first time in the history of the award that the recipient's work was not based solely on mathematical formulas, but instead considered the emotions of investors. Khaneman challenged the assumption that investors act rationally with their investment decisions. Again the irrational behavior of many investors is seen from studying of the Dalbar table and the Greed & Fear graph.

The evidence is very strong that a very good globally-diversified portfolio performs very well over time. That does not mean such a portfolio will have positive returns each and every year.

According to an April 21, 2015, article by ThinkAdvisor[9], President and CEO of Dalbar, Lou Harvey concluded this about the most recent study: "We all need a hand to hold at some point." Harvey further suggested "…that advisors needed not only to educate investors that markets will have periods of loses but more importantly, when those times occur, advisors must have a calming message ready to deliver and it must be delivered post haste."

Focus

"Convictions are more dangerous foes of truth than lies."
- Friedrich Nietzsche

Recently, I came across the quote above by Nietzsche.

---

8 http://www.nobelprize.org/nobel_prizes/economic-sciences/laureates/2002/kahneman-facts.html

9 http://www.thinkadvisor.com/2015/04/21/bad-behavior-cost-mutual-fund-investors-8-percentage points

I began to think about how it relates to investing and working with clients and prospects. I know that the Golden Rule of Investing is simple. I know that track record investing, market timing, and stock-picking are all examples of gambling and speculating with your money and NOT the definition of investing. I know that in any one year the majority of money managers do not "beat the market" and their ability to do so consistently year in and year out is impossible. I know that identifying those managers who will beat the market this year or next is not known before the fact.

Despite all the demonstrable academic evidence, you will always encounter prospects who have convictions; convictions that the market is rigged and can be beaten; convictions that five-star funds as rated by Morningstar are the road to success; convictions that cousin Vinny gets great tips on horses and stocks; convictions that someone or a group knows what XYZ stock is going to do next week.

For you to be successful investor, GET RID OF THOSE CONVICTIONS AND PUT YOUR EMOTIONS ON THE BACK BURNER.

CHAPTER 5
Successful Investing

"The four most expensive words in the English language are "This time it's different."
- John Templeton

Once you accept that stock-picking, market timing, and track record investing are simply ways that you or your advisor speculate and gamble with your money, you are well on your way to becoming a successful investor.

In addition, you need to adopt the investment philosophy that the markets are efficient. That does not mean the markets are without flaws. There will always be someone (or a group) that will do something dishonest. And for a short period of time, that dishonesty could disrupt the price of a stock. However, the good news is it will not last long.

Here are a couple of items to keep in mind on your investment journey. Prices in the market are set by the actions of the seven billion people on earth. Not buying a product affects the company that sells the product. It affects it in a negative way. Buying the product affects the company in a positive way. When a product is purchased, it represents an exchange between a willing buyer and a willing seller.

The talking heads on TV are fond of giving their opinions as to why the market went up or down today; oil prices were up, or the jobs reports did not meet expectations, or the Fed decided not to raise interest rates. I am sure that the market on any given day might have been influenced by some of those factors. But what really influences the market every day are the decisions of those seven billion humans. Every day, week, or month, the money from 401(k)s flow into or out of the market. Money flows out of the market every business day for Required Minimum Distributions (RMDs). Money flows into and out of mutual funds. Some individuals become so afraid of what they think is going to happen that they take all their money out of the market. Another group of individuals think just the opposite and buys into the market. Remember that in every trade there is a buyer and seller. Each of them thinks that their decision is correct or necessary. That is the basis of a free market. That is how the market works!

Setting up Your Portfolio

The evidence that stock picking, market timing, and track record investing do not work is strong. Knowing that reveals the answer as to how to invest.

- Since stock picking does not work, you should own the market.
- Since market timing does not work, you should stay in the market because historically-the market eventually goes up.
- Since track record investing does not work, you should ignore past performance.

Remember, as I have said before, the rules for investing are simple, but following them is not easy.

We also know from Fama & French that stocks have a risk premium over fixed income, value stocks have a risk premium over growth stocks and small stocks have a risk premium over large stocks.

Finally we know that by adding fixed income, particularly short term fixed income, we dampen the ups and downs of the portfolio. It lowers the value of the standard deviation.

There is only one other fact that you need to know to be a successful investor; PATIENCE!

Investing is a journey, not a sprint. That is all you need to know to be a successful investor. Honestly, that's it!

Putting it all Together

To own the market you have the following options:

- Use a number of mutual funds.
- Use a number of Exchange Traded Funds (EFTs).
- Use a combination of mutual funds and ETFs.
- Use individual stocks.
- Build a structured portfolio.

An equity mutual fund is a basket of stocks that is managed by a professional money manager. The stocks in a mutual fund will represent the goal of the money manager. For example, the fund could contain all large cap value stocks in the United States or all the energy stocks in North America. Another might be an index fund that tries to emulate the S&P 500 Index or the index of small cap stocks. ETFs are available that do the same thing. ETFs have lower costs than mutual funds and are traded like individual stocks.

The advantage of mutual funds and ETFs is that you can own anywhere from a few stocks to thousands of stocks thereby achieving a degree of diversification with one purchase. Since there are mutual funds and ETFs that represent almost every sector of the market, domestic and international, you could build a portfolio that owns the market and tilts toward value and small stocks.

Short term fixed income mutual funds are available as are fixed income Exchanged Traded Funds. Therefore you can construct a portfolio that fits your risk tolerance.

A structured portfolio can also be constructed using index type mutual funds. Investors cannot own an index, but you can own a surrogate. Index mutual funds have a couple of disadvantages. First, if a company offers a mutual fund that tracks an S&P 500 Index, it will manage it to follow the S&P 500 as closely as possible. It will not own all 500 stocks of the Index. That would be too expensive. Some years they will track the index more closely than other years. The difference between what the mutual fund returns, versus what the index actually returned, is called **tracking error**. Some index funds do better than others.

The second problem is that each year some new stocks are added to the S&P 500 Index and some are subtracted. When this happens, Standard & Poor's announces in advance which stocks will be moving into the index and which stocks will be dropped. This allows for arbitrage and a slight disruption in the index. It can affect mutual funds that follow the index.

One way to avoid the issues with strict indices is to create an index type fund that does not adhere to a specific number. Dimensional Fund Advisors (DFA) has done this for years. Instead of having a fund that tries to track the S&P 500 Index, DFA has a fund that represents the largest capitalized funds in the United States. That fund might contain 507 stocks or 490 or 598. The important point is that it tracks the same sector of stocks as does the S&P 500. That way, DFA avoids tracking error and the necessity of moving stocks in and out as is required of a mutual fund that attempts to track an index.

Further, Dimensional Fund Advisors takes the same approach with all of its funds. It allows DFA to create funds that focus on specific sectors, allowing them to be able to laser in on value and small and even microcap stocks (the smallest of the small) funds, using information from The Center for Research in Security Prices (CRSP), which we discussed earlier in Chapter 4, the Academic Approach to Investing.

Dimensional Fund Advisors was founded in 1981 by David G Booth and Rex Sinquefield, each of whom received advanced degrees from the University of Chicago and studied under Eugene Fama. Professor Fama sits on the board of DFA.[1]

Focus

Now that you understand that some degree of a globally diversified portfolio can be constructed using mutual funds, ETF, individual stocks (if you have enough money to truly diversify) and index type funds as offered by Dimensional Fund Advisers. I can tell you that using the latter allows more diversity in the portfolio and that is the method I use in constructing portfolios for my clients. However, there are circumstances when achieving diversity will not work. For example, when clients ask me to manage their 401(k)s, I am forced to use only those funds available in their retirement plan. In many instances, constructing a portfolio with real diversification is impossible; the funds offered do not cover all the asset classes needed for global diversification. I am sometimes successful when the client has other investments in addition to the 401(k) to make their entire investment portfolio truly diversified.

---

1 https://en.wikipedia.org/wiki/DimensionalFundAdvisors

In our next chapter, I am going to concentrate on the unique challenges that owners of small businesses face. You may want to skip it if you do not own your own business. If you are thinking about starting your own business or want to pick up a couple tips on how to save on taxes, by all means stay with me.

CHAPTER 6
Small Business Owners

"However difficult life may seem, there is always something you can do and succeed at."
- Stephen Hawking

I struggled with how to present this chapter. Much of it is based on a white paper I wrote for owners of small businesses on how they were making serious mistakes in not taking advantage of those pages in the tax code that were beneficial to their bottom line.

I finally reached the conclusion that following the format I used for the white paper was the best to use here. So here we go.

One of highest costs of the small business owner is taxes. And one of the best ways that a small business owner can improve their bottom line is to reduce taxes. It takes planning to reduce taxes and the month of April when your tax filing for the previous year is due, is way too late to do almost anything for last year. May first of this year is the time to plan tax savings for this year while the pain of that check you sent to the IRS is still fresh in your mind.

TAX PLANNING is NOT TAX PREPARATION

TAX PREPARATION is what your CPA does in the spring every year so that you are in compliance with the tax filing sections of the IRS code.

TAX PLANNING is what goes on throughout the year so that your CPA prepares your return such that you use all the rules in the IRS code to pay the minimum taxes each and every year. There are seventy-three-thousand pages in the tax code. A number of those pages contain ways small business owners can use those sections of the code to their advantage. In addition to the tax code, there is tax law. Tax law is often settled when cases are decided in court and sections of the code are clarified.

The most difficult aspect of tax planning is getting to the truth. It is easy to get opinions on tax questions. It is hard to get facts. But the facts do exist and you find the facts in the tax code and previously settled IRS cases.

Most small business owners believe in their CPAs. I know a couple of CPAs who do outstanding tax planning for their clients and I know a lot of CPAs who prepare their client's tax returns efficiently. But efficient tax preparation is not tax planning.

This is not a knock on CPAs. No one likes receiving a letter from the IRS questioning their latest tax return. The correct numbers belong in the correct box on the correct tax form. CPAs are educated and trained as accountants. That is what the "A" in CPA stands for—Accountant. An accountant keeps track of what happened. What happened is **history**. To save on taxes, planning ahead for the **future** is required, so that in the end, you control as much of the history as possible. William Hall III, titled one of his posts on LinkedIn "**There is not ONE question on the CPA exam about tax planning.**"[1]

---

1 https://www.linkedin.com/pulse/one-question-cpa-exam-tax-planning-hall-iii-l-i-o-n-open-network

Here are some of the mistakes that small business owners make.

MISTAKE #1 There is nothing the small business owner can do about minimizing taxes. Not true! There are steps you can take to reduce your taxes. There are a few of those 73,000 pages in the IRS code that benefit small owners. If there are pages in the code that offer a benefit, why wouldn't you use them?

MISTAKE #2 Your CPA is a great tax planner and knows the tax code. For the most part not true! There is no way to translate Certified Public Account into Tax Planner, or Tax Preparer, or Tax Guru, or tax anything. Are there exceptions? Sure, but the average CPA focuses on putting the right figures in the correct boxes on the tax form and making sure the forms are filed on time. With such a complicated tax code, we Small Business Owners need professionals who make sure that what is entered is correct. More importantly, we need professionals who are claiming every single deduction that the law allows. The emphasis is on "What is allowed." We are not talking about doing anything illegal, immoral, or unethical.

MISTAKE #3 The Home Office Deduction is a red flag for audit. Definitely not true! The IRS gives us two ways to describe how to deduct expenses for the use of a home office. If the IRS outlines two ways to calculate the deductions for using your home office, how can it be a red flag, if you follow their instructions? Answer: IT IS NOT A RED FLAG. There is also tax law. Tax law can be used in your favor. There was a case of a doctor who deducted the office where he met with patients, his home office where he prepared paperwork, and a home office in his vacation home. The IRS sued him and LOST. This is an example of Case Law. Looking at the details of Case Law allows all tax preparers to use it for their clients.

MISTAKE #4 "How Much you Make" is more important than "How Much You Keep." Only partly true! It is HOW you make it that determines how much you keep. The operative word is HOW. Different entities are taxed at different rates. How you are organized now and in the future means TAX PLANNING is key.

MISTAKE #5 Tax Planning is not worth my time; my income is too high to save anything with Tax Planning. Definitely NOT true! Actually the more you make, the greater the opportunities that are available to you in the area of tax savings. If you reduce your tax burden by $20,000, that is $20,000 that you already earned and have in your pocket. To earn enough to keep $20,000, you might have to increase your sales by $80,000. Gross $80,000, net $35,000, pay taxes of $15,000 and you have $20,000 in your pocket! It is well worth your while to look into how to do some tax planning. It could be a whole lot easier to discover how to keep $20,000 that is already in your pocket than to increase your sales.

A colleague of mine, John Pollack, has started a firm in Allen, Texas which addresses the missed tax saving opportunities that small business owners are not taking even though they are clearly printed in the IRS code. Financial Gravity works with small business owners, allowing you to take back to your CPA, tax deductions that they have missed so that you keep more of your hard earned money.[2] The focus is on tax deductions that are;

1. Legal-Listed in the code or decided by Case Law.
2. Ethical-Doing nothing that is shady.
3. Moral-Some things are legal but not moral.

---

2 Financial Gravity's Tax BluePrint® https://financialgravity.com/

There are Only Four Ways to Address Tax Savings—Only Four!

This is not the final four, it is the **Only Four**. Think of it this way; there are only three primary colors, but endless shades and color combinations. There are 12 notes in a scale, but an endless number of songs and scores. In reverse, there are 73,000 pages in the tax code, but there are only four basic strategies in dealing with taxes.

1. **Shifting:** We can shift the flow of money from a business entity or person to a different business entity or person. I gave a couple of examples of shifting earlier in the book, but did not use that term. The use of Roth IRAs, 529 Plans, Health Savings Accounts (HSAs) and cash value life insurance are all examples of shifting. Each of them is covered in the 73,000 pages of the tax code. We will discuss some of these ideas in Chapter 10.
2. **Timing:** You can't time the stock market and be successful over the long term, but you can time the tax code. Putting pre-tax money in a Traditional IRA or a 401(k) is a timing strategy. You avoid taxes now, but pay them later. Tax avoidance is legal. Using the tax code to your advantage is TAX AVOIDANCE. TAX EVATION, on the other hand, is illegal. Don't do something illegal.
3. **Tax Code:** The 73,000 pages of information in the tax code is not a secret. It is written and published for everyone to read. It allows some to write off a swimming pool; you can rent your home to yourself; you can get a better write-off for leasing a car and no write-off for buying a car. None of it is logical, but all of it is written into the Internal Revenue Code. **By following the code you can save thousands of dollars. By ignoring the code you can waste thousands of dollars. Your choice!!**

4. **Products:** Most products fall into one of the strategies listed. I mentioned cash value life insurance under shifting. To choose a product because it is allowed by the tax code may not be the best choice for the long term. Here is an example. In the 1980s the Congress of the United States decided that investors were being sold "investments" that were not really investments at all but rather ways to take advantage of a section of the tax code. The "investment" allowed tax deductions that had little to do with investment risk. Rather, the product gave the investor a deduction for a risk, that for the most part, did not exist. Therefore, it was not an investment. It was a tax shelter. Investors who bought those products thinking they were investments for the long term suffered when Congress canceled them retroactively. It is important to use products that are not only right for you and your situation now, but ones that you believe will be around for the long term.

Who Benefits Most from Tax Planning?

Does serious tax planning work for all small business owners? The more money your business earns and taxes you pay, opens more opportunities for tax savings. Almost any small business that makes a profit can save taxes by using a SIMPLE plan for their retirement as well as for their employees.

Here is a rule of thumb that you can use to determine if your business can save **serious** tax dollars:

- The business generates taxable income of $80,000 annually.
- The business pays more than $20,000 annually in taxes.

If your business meets the two criterions above, I encourage you to contact me through my website www.savinginvestors.com and request a free consultation. My goal in chatting with you would be to see if I can offer you some business planning advice that will save you money.

Sale of Your Business as Your Sole Retirement Account

The sale of a successful business can provide for a comfortable retirement. However, putting all your eggs in that basket could be a mistake. The timing of your retirement might turn out to be a bad time to sell the business. Worse yet, the growth potential of the business might be out of favor at the moment you want to retire. Opening a store to rent movie DVDs looked like a good business until Netflix came along.

To bridge the gap, you can use some of the tax savings available for business owners while you are still managing your business. Part of these funds could be used to increase your contributions to whichever retirement plan you created for your business. Having a contingency plan makes sense.

Focus

The purpose of this chapter is to alert you that in those 73,000 pages of the IRS code there is enough help that you should be putting it to work in your TAX PLANNING. Talk to your CPA sometime between May 1 and September 15 and ask lots of questions: Is the business entity I am using the correct one? Can I hire my kids? What is the best retirement plan for me? The IRS deserves respect; it is not to be feared. I will give you more tax saving ideas in Chapter 10.

CHAPTER 7

Retirement Savings, College Funding, Health Savings Accounts and Other Goals

"In general, saving for retirement should be your top priority. As the standard advice goes, you can always borrow for college, but there are no loans to pay for retirement."
- Joan Bodnar Kiplinger Magazine

There are many reasons to save, but there are two long-term goals for most investors; retirement and college funding. Unfortunately, the two can create real conflicts for parents.

Most people want to help their children get a good education. The cost of college today is over the moon. Here is a truth that you may not want to face. Unless you start saving for retirement immediately upon receiving your first pay check, and open a college funding account on the day your children are born, the probability of achieving both goals is minimal.

There are exceptions, such as generous grandparents and kids with good work and savings "genes." The bottom line is this: YOU WILL RETIRE, SO BEST YOU SAVE FOR THOSE RETIREMENT YEARS. Retirement needs to be your first goal.

Because of a number of advancements in the last few decades, Americans spend more years in retirement than ever before. In fact, planning for a retirement of 25-35 years is a must. That will be 25-35 years without a paycheck. That number of years in retirement can be a scary thought. If there is longevity in your family, plan for a *very long* time in retirement.

Investing for Retirement

If you work at a company that offers a retirement plan such as a 401(k) or a 403b, and it has a matching feature, you should enroll in the program immediately. You should contribute up to the match. Here is an example of how it works:

1. Big Company hires you at a salary of $50,000 per year.
2. Big Company matches 50% of your contribution, up to 6% of your salary.
3. You sign up to contribute 6% of your salary or $3,000 per year.
4. Big Company matches 50% or $1,500.
5. Total annual contribution to your 401(k) plan is $4,500.

If you contribute 10% of your salary or $5,000 per year, Big Company will still only pay $1,500. Why only contribute up to the match? I discuss that in Chapter 10 when I reveal **Investing Traps**. Suffice to say, that the more money you have at the time of retirement in accounts that have never been taxed, the bigger your tax bill during retirement.

Your target for savings should be a minimum of 10% of your income; 15% is a better target. Going back to the example of the Big Company 401(k), and a salary of $50,000, you should be saving $5,000 to $7,500 per year. In the example given, you save 9%, including the company match. Where should you be saving the remaining $3,000 to get to $7,500? It should go into a Roth IRA. Roth IRAs are funded with after-tax money, grow tax deferred, and are available for distribution after age 59 ½. Those distributions are tax free under the current tax code. The reason for using a Roth IRA as an investment vehicle becomes more apparent when we get to Chapters 10 and 11.

What if your company offers a 401(k) or other retirement plan, but does not offer a match? Then the first $5,500 dollars (max contribution for those less than 50 years old) should go into a Roth and the next $2,000 should go into the 401(k).

I often hear the complaint that says "I can't afford that." If you want to retire comfortably, you can't afford not to. The first step to take is to have savings taken out of your check automatically. That is easy with company plans because contributions are automatically deducted from gross pay. Payments to a Roth IRA can also be made automatically. Suppose you get paid twice a month. Your check is automatically deposited into your checking account on the 1st and the 15th of each month. Set up an automatic transfer out of your checking account on the 2nd and 16th of each month to the Roth account. It is easy to accomplish.

Why invest automatically? Because you will be much more likely to invest and live on the take-home amount of your income as opposed to spending first and saving what is left over. This is a case where what you don't see will help you.

And finally, when you get a raise, increase your investment amount by 25% of the amount of the raise. Make that a life time practice and your retirement goals will become easier to achieve.

Self-employed individuals have plans they can use for retirement investments. There are SIMPLE plans (**S**avings **I**ncentive **M**atch **P**lans), Individual 401(k) plans, Simplified Employee Pension plans (SEPS), Defined Benefit plans (DB) and a few others. It is not the intent of this book to provide the pros and cons of each of these plans. For information on retirement plans go to ww.irs.gov and search "retirement plans." IRS Pub 560 is a good starting place for owners of small businesses.

As I stated earlier, the self-employed should avoid planning on building a business with its main goal being the profit from the sale of the business funding their retirement years. That is an example of putting all your eggs in one basket. In addition to your business you should be investing somewhere outside the business itself. Put an expense line in your Income Statement called "Retirement Fund."

Investing for College

Every state in the Union offers 529 Plans. You as a parent invest after tax money in mutual type funds offered by a state plan. Earnings grow tax deferred and are not subject to federal tax and generally not subject to state tax when the proceeds are used for qualified educational expenses of the designated beneficiary of the plan (the student). The proceeds can be used for college and/or other post-secondary training. Contributions to 529 plans are not tax deductible. You do not have to be a resident of the state in order to contribute to that state's 529 Plan. For example, a resident of Virginia can open the 529 plan offered by the state of Utah. However, the Virginia resident will not receive a tax credit on their Virginia state tax return. Residents of Utah who open the Utah 529 plan do receive a small tax credit on their Utah tax return. With some limitations, beneficiaries can be changed in 529 plans and there is no time limit in moving the money out of a 529 plan. Funds removed from a 529 plan not used for qualified educational expenses will generally be taxed at ordinary tax rates PLUS a 10% penalty. State taxes may also be due. In addition to information on the IRS website, www.irs.gov, you can also find more details at www.savingforcollege.com.

Health Saving Accounts-Tax Free Money

There are very few IRS options that allow for workers to earn money and not pay taxes on those earnings. This is especially true for W-2 earners; those who work for someone else and receive a pay check. Health Savings Accounts is one of those exceptions.

Health Savings Accounts (HSA) are available to employees who have a health insurance policy with a high deductible. The Internal Revenue Service defines "high deductible" as a minimum of $1,300 for a policy covering one person and a minimum of $2,600 for a policy that covers a family. The meaning of "deductible" is the amount of out of pocket dollars that a purchaser of a policy must pay each year before the insurance company will pay its share.

Here is an example. Suppose you purchase a medical insurance policy which agrees to pay for 80% of all claims and you are responsible for 20% with a deductible of $1,300. Suppose you were riding your bicycle, had an accident and ended up in the emergency room. The cost of the emergency visit is $2,375. Here is how the bill would be covered for your first claim.

Out of Pocket Expenses	
Cost of Emergency Room Visit	$2,375
Your Deductible for First Claim	$1,300
Balance	$1,075
Insurance Company Pays 80%	$860
Your 20% Responsibility	$215
YOUR TOTAL COST	$1,515

The bad news is that you have to come up with $1,515 to pay the emergency room bill. The good news is that for the rest of the year your cost will be only 20% of the bill. One final note on how medical policies work. The higher the deductible, the lower will be the monthly premium all other things being equal. The maximum deductible for 2016 for self-only coverage is $6,550 and $13,100 for family coverage.

The Role of Health Savings Accounts

For 2016, a single person can contribute $3,350 to an HSA while a family can contribute up to $6,750. Those amounts can be increased by $1,000 for those 55 and older. The amount of money contributed to an HSA is tax free-you get to deduct it on your tax return. In our example about the bicycle accident, if a Health Savings Account were in place, the $1,515 could be paid out of the HSA account. You get to pay medical bills with tax free money. There is no tax on money taken from an HSA account to pay medical bills!

Funds that are not used in any one calendar year remain in the account. If you put $3,000 in a self-only HSA for three years in a row and never had to use any of it, you would have $9,000. Health Savings Accounts do not earn much in the way of interest but that is not important in the long term.

There are a number of restrictions around the use of HSAs. None of them are draconian. One restriction is that you cannot contribute to a Health Savings Account if you are covered by Medicare. But that does not mean you can't have funds in an HSA that was established prior to your coverage by Medicare. Ironically, you can use money in the HSA to pay for Part B of your Medicare premium. That runs about $105 per month. Think of it as a type of Roth IRA, targeted for Medicare premiums, where you can pay premiums with tax free money.

Focus

In life you will always face a series of conflicts. Many will be easy to resolve. Others such as how you will save for retirement while also saving for your children's college education can be daunting. If you start early, save first, invest wisely and spend what is left while investing wisely, you have a reasonable chance of success. If you ignore any of these four options you will have a difficult time achieving both of these goals. It is important to understand that someday you will retire without a paycheck for 20-30 years. Social Security alone will not afford you a comfortable retirement. There are other ways for your young adult(s) to achieve a college diploma. Jobs are scarce for you when you reach seventy-five or eighty years of age. You are not being selfish putting your retirement needs first. Working for forty or fifty years deserves some kind of reward.

PART TWO
THE SPENDING YEARS
The Decent Down the Mountain

CHAPTER 8
Preparing for Retirement and the Retirement Years

"My parents didn't want to move to Florida, but they turned 60, and that's the law."

- Jerry Seinfeld

Focusing on saving and investing is not all you need to do in order to be ready for retirement. Once you automate the investment portion, there are a few other items that need attention.

The Empty Nest Years

Your kids are grown and graduated from college or have entered their own working years. Your expenses have dropped and you have an opportunity to put more money into your retirement accounts. Most people don't take advantage of this unexpected opportunity. In a recent white paper entitled *Do Households Save More When the Kids Leave Home?* May 2016, from the Center for Retirement Research at Boston College,[1] they found that;

- Parents have more money to spend or save.
- Tax data analysis shows they save only slightly more in 401(k)s, but far below what is needed for a secure retirement.
- Parents spend most of the additional funds that become available.

1 Do Households Save More When the Kids Leave Home? May 2016, from the Center for Retirement Research at Boston College

Budgets

Most people hate budgets, but if you do not consider the income and expenses that change from the working years to the retirement years, you may set yourself up for failure. There are many free budget plans on line.[2] When I talk to clients about how their life changes as they move into retirement, one of their first things they say is, "My expenses will be lower. I won't be driving to work. In fact, we may not even need two cars. In addition, my clothing bill will be much lower as my need for suits disappears." My answer to these clients is this: You may be right, but let's talk about what you *will be* doing in your first five to 10 years in retirement. Here are some of the items that come up in our discussion:

- Leisure travel to places we always wanted to visit.
- Eating out more often.
- Taking classes that I have always wanted to but never had the time.
- Spending more time with the grandchildren (who often live across the country), which equals more travel.
- Helping adult children in need.
- Aiding grandchildren in college.

After a while, it becomes clear that a lot of the savings that were associated with job expenses will be eaten up with a new to-do list of activities. Don't ignore putting pen to paper to map out all your income and expenses for your new life style.

2 http://www.goodfinancialcents.com/best-free-online-budgeting-tools/

Retiring in a New Location

Many individuals and couples plan on retiring in a new state, city, or possibly a different country from where they have spent their working years. Moving to a new area is expensive. It becomes even more expensive if after six months in the new home you find you made a big mistake. This happens often when you vacation in the same area year after year and decide that is where you will retire. Perhaps you go to the same beach for every vacation or maybe to the same ski town. What happens in vacation towns during the vacation time of year is not the same as living in that town 52 weeks a year.

My wife, Carole was born and raised in Southern California. I was born and raised in the East, where the seasons are more apparent. We lived and worked in the L.A. area but spent many of our vacations skiing in Park City, Utah. We decided to move to Park City, but years before we did, we visited Park City and the surrounding areas in the spring, summer, and fall, which were the seasons we missed when we spent ski vacations there. We subscribed to the local newspaper to determine how the local governments operated and read the letters to the editor to get an idea of how the locals thought about issues.

After all that, THEN we moved to Park City.

Everything has worked out very well for us. I must share with you one item that did have me concerned. Carole moved to Park City four months before I did. She arrived in September and I arrived full time in January. Snow begins to fall as early as October. November can dump some pretty good snow storms. It is one thing to love fresh snow when you are in town for a ski vacation. It is quite another to wake and have to clear six to eight inches from a long driveway while it is still snowing, and then discover that the rear wheel drive car does not operate real well on snow packed roads. I never received the dreaded phone call that was in my mind from Carole telling me to come and take her back to L.A. ASAP!

Changes in Expenses as Retirement Progresses

After a decade of traveling, eating out a couple of times a week, and catching up on those education courses you missed earlier in life, as well as helping adult children and grandchildren, things tend to slow down a little. Your tendency is to stay closer to home and spend more time with friends you made in the last decade. Although you may still be doing some travelling, it is not as extensive as it was in the early days. You start to recognize your own aging. Suddenly, you notice you can't do all the things you used to do, particularly in areas requiring strength and endurance. More importantly, more doctor visits become a necessity. The tendency is to settle into a more leisurely style of living. Even with higher medical expenses, your finances do not tend to be an issue early on.[3]

However, as you progress into your 80s and 90s, the cost of medical care becomes a bigger expense item in your budget. The 2016 Health View Services Retirement Health Care Costs Data Report was released in May 2016.[4] Here are a few highlights:

- An average healthy 65-year-old couple retiring in 2016 is projected to spend $288,400 on lifetime Medicare Parts B, D and supplemental insurance (Plan F) premiums.
- The cost of dental, hearing, vision and all other out-of-pocket expenses are an additional $89,012.

---

3 http://money.usnews.com/money/blogs/the-smarter-mutual-fund-investor/2014/08/22/3-stages-of-saving-and-spending-in-retirement

4 http://www.prnewswire.com/news-releases/healthview-services-2016-retirement-health-care-costs-data-report-released-300270880.html

- A 66-year-old couple retiring in 2016 will spend 57% of their Social Security benefits to cover all medical costs in retirement.
- A 55-year-old couple retiring in 10 years will spend 88% of their Social Security benefits to cover all medical costs in retirement.
- A 45-year-old couple retiring in 20 years will spend 116% of their Social Security benefits to cover all medical costs in retirement.

The calculations are based on Social Security projections of a 3.1% cost of living adjustment (COLA) in 2017 and 2.7% thereafter. Looking at the big increase from using 57% of the Social Security benefit to cover medical costs in retirement for those retiring this year, versus using all of the benefits plus another 16% for those retiring in 20 years, says that Social Security benefits will not cover medical costs in retirement years. Why? Because the cost of inflation in health care during retirement out-paces the increases in Social Security benefits. As a result, more and more of the Social Security benefit is spent on health care.

The implication of these findings, particularly for those retiring in 10 years and later, is huge. It says there will be little to nothing left from your Social Security benefit check after paying medial costs. It means more retirement savings is essential *if* those who are more than ten years away from retirement expect to live comfortably.

There is much more in the report and I suggest you read at least the press release that is referenced in footnote 4 for this chapter. From a retirement standpoint, you need only understand what I have included here.

Many people 45 and younger often tell me not to include Social Security benefits when I prepare a financial plan for them. I follow their instructions, but I always show the plan with Social Security benefits as well as without benefits. Every wage earner in the United States pays Federal Insurance Contributions Act (FICA) taxes. For everyone, 6.2% of their salary is the Social Security tax, and 1.45% is the Medicare tax, for a total of 7.65%. The wage earner pays that amount and the employer pays the same amount, for a total FICA tax of 15.3%. There are no plans by the federal government to stop collecting the FICA tax. I believe Social Security benefits will be available in 20-plus years. I also believe there will be changes. Presently anyone born in 1960 or later do not reach their full retirement age until their age 67. That age may increase in the future. Plus, the tax percentage may increase from 7.65% for both the employer and employee to who-knows-what? Only time will tell.

And finally, if you think you can automatically depend on Medicare, think again. Medicare is totally different from Social Security, as are the qualifications. To qualify for Medicare you need to be:

- At least 65 years old.
- A United States citizen or legal resident who has lived in the United States for a minimum of five years.
- A worker who worked for a Medicare-covered employer for at least 10 years.

If you are eligible for Medicare and do not have medical insurance from an employer, failure to apply for Medicare coverage during your enrollment window, will result in a penalty that will continue for all the years you collect Medicare. Your enrollment window begins three months before you turn 65, the month of your 65th birthday and the three months after the month of your sixty fifth birthday, www.medicare.gov

In Chapter 11, we will come back to Medicare to discuss costs and the importance of you planning EACH year and your sources of income. Failure to do so will decrease your spendable income.

Focus

It is just as important to plan non-financial issues for your years in retirement as well as those that deal with money. You may plan to stay in your present home so you are not worried about moving to a new location; but have you thought about climbing stairs when you are 83? The real purpose of this chapter has been to widen your thought process about your relaxing years. After all, it will probably last a third of your lifetime.

CHAPTER 9
Social Security

"Should any political party attempt to abolish Social Security, unemployment insurance, and eliminate labor laws and farm programs, you would not hear of that party again in our political history."
- Dwight D. Eisenhower

Social Security benefits can turn out to be one of your most valuable assets in retirement. By itself it will not be enough to live on, but as part of your retirement plan it can make the difference between a very comfortable existence and just an okay existence after you leave the workforce.

The Basics for Social Security Benefits

To qualify for benefits, a person must first have been issued a Social Security number. To receive a number, the person does not have to be a citizen of the United States. They only have to be in the country legally and have the right to work.

Every person who has worked and earned a qualifying salary for 40 quarters is eligible for benefits. One quarter is defined as earning $1,260 in one calendar year for 2016. An employee can only earn four quarters in any one calendar year. Therefore, anyone who earns $5,040 in 2016 will be credited with four quarters of Social Security credit. It does not matter if the $5,040 is earned in the first week of the year or the last week of the year or throughout the year.

In order to earn 40 quarters, a person must have a work record of a minimum of 10 years. A worker can earn fewer than four quarters in any year, but as long as they earn a total of 40 quarters of credits, they qualify for Social Security benefits.

You calculate the value of your benefit by taking the highest 35 years of benefits (some of those years might only contain earnings from one or two quarters). If a worker qualifies with 40 quarters, but fewer than 35 years, each year without earnings is counted as zero.

The formula that the Social Security Administration uses is complicated. Among other issues, it takes into account the national wage index each year. For example, $15,000 earned in 1986 is counted differently from $15,000 earned in 2015[1] due to cost-of-living increases.

Collecting Benefits

The earliest a worker can claim benefits is age 62. The longer a worker delays benefits, the higher the benefit will be up to age 70. There is no benefit increase past age 70. Here is a table of benefit amounts at various ages.[2]

1 https://www.ssa.gov/OACT/COLA/QC.html

2 https://www.ssa.gov/planners/retire/agereduction.html

Social Security Benefits Are Reduced When Claiming Early

Year of Birth[1]	Full (normal) Retirement Age	Months between age 62 and full retirement age[2]	At Age 62[3]			
			A $1000 retirement benefit would be reduced to	The retirement benefit is reduced by[4]	A $500 spoues's benefit would be reduced to	The spouse's benefit is reduced by[5]
1937 or earlier	65	36	$800	20.00%	$375	25.00%
1938	65 & 2 months	38	$791	20.83%	$370	25.83%
1939	65 & 4 months	40	$783	21.67%	$366	26.67%
1940	65 & 6 months	42	$775	22.50%	$362	27.50%
1941	65 & 8 months	44	$766	23.33%	$358	28.33%
1942	65 & 10 months	46	$758	24.17%	$354	29.17%
1943-1954	66	48	$750	25.00%	$350	30.00%
1955	66 & 2 months	50	$741	25.83%	$345	30.83%
1956	66 & 4 months	52	$733	26.67%	$341	31.67%
1957	66 & 6 months	54	$725	27.50%	$337	32.50%
1958	66 & 8 months	56	$716	28.33%	$333	33.33%
1959	66 & 10 months	58	$708	29.17%	$329	34.17%
1960 and later	67	60	$700	30.00%	$325	35.00%

1. *If you were born on January 1st, you should refer to the previous year.*
2. *If you were born on the 1st of the month, we figure your benefit (and your full retirement age) as if your birthday was in the previous month. If you were born on January 1st, we figure your benefit (and your full retirement age) as if your birthday was in December of the previous year.*
3. *You must be at least 63 for the entire month to receive benefits*
4. *The maximum benefit for the spouse is 50% of the benefit the worker would receive at full retirement age. The % reduction for the spouse should be applied after the automatic 50% reduction.*
5. *Percentages are due to rounding.*

Find the year in which you were born, the first column in the chart, and then look at column two. That is the age at which you qualify for what is called your Full Retirement Benefit. It is also referred to as your Full Retirement Age (FRA). For every year you postpone taking your Social Security benefit beyond your Full Retirement Age, your benefit increases by 8%. For anyone born between 1943 and 1954, inclusive, their benefit increases by 32% if they wait to take their benefit at their age 70.

If you were born in 1950, you reach your Full Retirement Age, 66, in 2016. If your benefit is $2,000 per month starting in 2016, by delaying benefits until you reach age 70 in 2020, you will receive a benefit of $2,640 per month ($2,000.00 times 1.32).

By the same token, for each year you apply early, that is before you reach your Full Retirement Age, your benefit is reduced. If you take your benefit at age 62 and your Full Retirement Age is 66 your benefit is reduced by 25%. The Social Security Administration will adjust the benefit proportionately when the date of filing is more or less than a year.

There are many other matters to consider other than at what age to file. For example, if you are married, when you file can affect your spouse's benefit when they file. It can also affect the benefit of a surviving widow or widower. There are benefits for dependent children under Social Security when a parent dies. It is not my intent to cover all areas of the Social Security Act. I have covered some of the major issues to consider. Suffice it to say that when and how you file for Social Security benefits should not be taken lightly.[3]

---

3 https://www.ssa.gov/

When and Why Delaying Benefits Makes Sense

Once you retire, you rely on Social Security, retirement accounts, saving accounts and possibly a pension. Pensions for the most part do not have cost-of-living adjustments, which means if you receive $750 on the first month of your retirement you will still receive $750 in month number 120, 10 years in the future. The purchasing power of $750 in the year 2026 will only buy about $558 worth of goods if inflation runs at 3% per year.

Most years, Social Security receives a cost-of-living adjustment (COLA). There have only been three years in the last 40 where Social Security recipients have not received a COLA; 2010, 2011 and 2016. There was no COLA for these three years because there was no increase in the Consumer Price Index (CPI-W) from the third quarter of the previous years. The Bureau of Labor Statistics (BLS) publishes the *Consumer Price Index for Urban Wage Earners and Clerical Workers* (CPI-W) on a monthly basis. The CPI-W is used to annually adjust benefits paid to Social Security beneficiaries and Supplemental Security Income recipients.[4]

For example for 2016, the CPI-W was flat from the third quarter of 2014 to the third quarter of 2015. Social Security recipient's find out in October of each year what the percent change in their benefit will be or not be, beginning the following January.

For 2017, the percent change is only 0.3%. The lowest increase ever, except for those 0% years.

4 https://www.ssa.gov/oact/STATS/cpiw.html

Here is a table that shows you what happens when a beneficiary takes benefits early, at their Full Retirement Age, and if they delay until age 70. Consider a person born in 1950 whose benefit at age 66, their Full Retirement Age, is $2,000 per month.

Monthly vs Annual Benefits

Age	Monthly Benefit	Annual Benefit
62	$1,500	$18,000
66	$2,000	$24,000
70	$2,640	$31,680

The difference between taking $18,000 a year at age 62 and $31,680 at age 70 is $13,680 or $1,140 per month. Over ten years that amounts to just under $137,000. The argument against waiting is that taking $18,000 per year at age 62 (we are ignoring COLAs for the ease of comparison) means an income of $144,000 over those 8 years versus waiting until you reach age 70.

There is a litigable argument to take your benefit early, but here is a key point worth considering. At retirement, your other retirement accounts (IRAs, ROTHs, 401(k)s, etc.) may be at their highest value. Your ability to work at least part time will more than likely be an option if more income is needed. As you reach your seventies and eighties, a bigger Social Security check will be very beneficial.

Also, consider how the cost-of-living adjustment works. If the COLA is 2%, the monthly increase on $1,500 would be $30 or $360 for the year. The increase on $2,640 is $52.80 per month or to $634 per year; $360 versus $634.

In an article in the August 22-26 2016 edition of Investment News by Elizabeth MacBride entitled *"Surviving Old Age,"* Charles D Ellis' book *"Falling Short"* is referenced. Ellis estimated in his book that the typical American worker could double their retirement savings from $100,000 to almost $250,000 simply by delaying taking Social Security until age 70 instead of beginning at age 62.[5]

Another reason to delay taking your Social Security benefit until age 70 is the fact that Americans are living longer. Based on an article by Paul Recer of ABC News, life expectancy for Americans age 65 in 2000 is 18 years, on average. In 1900, 65-year-olds could expect to live, on average, another 12 years. In 1998, women accounted for 58 percent of those over 65 and 70 percent of those 85 or older. About 41 percent of the older women live alone.[6]

You may have heard the standard advice as to how to take withdrawals from your retirement accounts. That is, avoid taking income from tax deferred accounts as long as possible. However, it may make sense to take some money from a tax deferred account in the early years of retirement so you can delay applying for Social Security benefits which will provide more income in your later retirement years. Each person's case is different, but in planning your leisure years, when to take your Social Security benefit should be one of your MAJOR DECISIONS.

---

5 http://www.investmentnews.com/article/20160822/FEATURE/160809926/the-longevity-paradox-as-americans-live-longer-they-run-the-risk-of

6 Collecting SS benefits prior to FRA limits the amount of money you can earn before your benefit will be reduced.

Focus

Years ago, a great many people retired at 65, lived on Social Security, a pension and whatever savings they were able to accumulate. Many, at least the male of the species, died in the next ten to fifteen years and the wife lived on the proceeds from a small life insurance policy plus Social Security. She received the higher of either her Social Security benefit or his, but now there is only one Social Security check arriving each month. That is the story of my parents. You must plan your decision to take your Social Security benefit carefully. If you want to know what your options are and how different scenarios will play out for you, contact me on my website; http://savinginvestors.com/.

CHAPTER 10
Investing Traps and Forgotten Expenses

"I'm proud to be paying taxes in the United States. The only thing is, I could be just as proud for half the money."
- Arthur Godfrey

We talked about being taken in by con men, prognosticators and gurus in Chapter 3, but there are a couple of subtle traps that await even the most successful investor who believes they have planned well for retirement. The biggest trap? TAXES!

For many years, the financial industry has provided rules of thumb for your retirement years. One that was, and still can be found today; you can retire on 75% of what you were earning in the last three to five years of employment. Another is that in retirement, you will be in a lower tax bracket than you were during your working years.

Perhaps you will be happy with living on 75% of what you were making in the last few working years, but maybe not. In the first 10 years of retirement, retirees tend to spend the most...except for maybe the last 10 years of retirement.

In the early few years of retirement retirees tend to take all those trips and vacations they put off while they had careers. Visits to grandchildren who live half way across the country are high on the list. Grandparents, especially grandma and grandchildren, get along really well according to the well-known fact; they have a common enemy. But after a while, as said earlier, travel tends to slow down a bit and spending levels off.

I will come back to why spending increases in the last 10 years of retirement a little later.

Taxes

Many, if not most, investment vehicles used for retirement involve the use of tax deferred 401(k)s or 403b(s) and traditional IRAs. All three of these plans provide tax breaks when money is invested. Contributions are tax deductible. The money grows tax deferred and is taxed at ordinary tax rates when distributed from the plan. When you reach the age of 70½, the law requires you to take money out of these plans whether or not you need the money. In the 1970s, Fram Oil Filters ran commercials where the tag line was "Pay me now or pay me later." That is what the IRS does with 401(k) plans and the like. IRAs were established in 1974 and 401(k)s in 1978. They were promoted then and are promoted now to avoid taxes now based on the belief that you will be in a lower tax bracket in retirement.

Do you believe that you will be in a lower tax bracket when you retire? True, some will be in a lower bracket, but maybe not you. In fact, I have not talked to anyone in recent years who believes that the tax rates in the future will be lower than they are today. The United States has a national debt closing in on twenty trillion dollars[1]. That is 20 followed by TWELVE ZEROS! In addition, politicians continue to run annual deficits and pat themselves on the back when the deficit goes down from one year to the next. All deficits add to the debt! Finally, when the Fed raises interest rates, that have been near zero since 2008, the service on the debt will increase. Too many

1 http://www.usdebtclock.org/

issues point to the higher probability that taxes will increase in the next few years to ignore the issue.

Here is an example of how taxes affect you when you withdraw funds from your tax deferred accounts. For the sake of simplicity, assume that all your tax deferred accounts have been consolidated in one traditional IRA. The only other funds available in retirement will be Social Security and some savings. The couple in the example is each 66 years old and their mortgage has been paid in full.

For an IRA with a value of $1,500,000 at retirement:

- Annual income desired from IRA is $100,000
- Present marginal tax brackets: Federal 25%, State 5%
- Income from Social Security, $2,500/month or $30,000/year

It looks like this couple is well set for a comfortable retirement. Let's take a look at what happens when we take taxes into account.

Without any serious deductions to use on their tax return, the couple takes the standard deduction and two personal exemptions on their annual income tax return. For the tax year 2016, the standard deduction is $15,100 for a married couple each of whom is 66 years of age and the personal exemption for each of them is $4,050. Therefore, the total deduction for the couple is $23,200. Here is what the taxes would look like;

1. Total Income $100,000 (from IRA) plus $30,000 (SS) = $130,000
2. Less: $23,100 standard deduction and personal exemption = $106,800
3. Less: $4,500 (only 85% of SS is taxable in this example) = $102,300 Taxable Amount
4. The Federal Tax on $102,300 for our couple is $17,118

5. The State Tax on $106,800 at 5% is $5,120 (could be slightly less depending on State deductions allowed.)
6. Total Income Tax is $22,308
7. Spendable Amount is $107,692[2]

Therefore, the couple in our example receives $130,000 but they don't have $130,000 to spend. They only have $107,692 to spend. Suppose the couple really planned on spending $130,000 each year. How much will they have to take from the IRA to have $130,000 to spend? The standard deduction and the personal exemptions will not change, nor will the taxable amount of Social Security in this new example.

The answer most people give is $22,308 because $130,000 minus $107,692 equals $22,308. That is not the correct answer because the extra $22,308 coming out of the IRA is all taxable at the 30% tax rate; 25% federal, and 5% state. The actual amount that must be taken from the IRA for the couple to have $130,000 of after tax spending money is $31,804. Here is how the numbers look when taxes are taken into account[3];

2 www.irs.gov calculations based on 2016 tax table

3 ibid

Spendable Income After Taxes

Distribution from IRA	$131,804
Income from Social Security	$30,000
Total Income	$161,804
Less Standard Deduction & Personal Exemptions	$23,100
Less Amount on Non-Taxable Social Security	$4,500
Taxable Amount	$134,204
Less Federal Tax at 28% Tax Bracket	$25,094
Less State Tax at 5%	$6,710
Spendable Income Before Expenses for Medicare Parts B & D	$130,000

The real question is "Did the couple plan on taking $131,804 out of their IRA in the first year of retirement so that they could spend $130,000?"

Here is another eye opener. If the couple did take $131,804 out of an IRA worth $1,500,000 in the first year it would be equal to a withdrawal rate of 8.79%. That is an unsustainable rate. Many advisors target a withdrawal rate of 4%, which would be $60,000 (4% of $1,500,000) and that would be before taxes.

Many retirees are upset when they find out that up to 85% of their Social Security income can be taxable. Further, the annual income from Social Security is $30,000 before any deductions for Medicare Parts B & D. Suppose the deductions for Medicare B & D amount to $450 per month. Remember both husband and wife is each receiving a Social Security check. Net income from the $2,500 monthly gross

Social Security checks will be $2,050 per month or $24,600 per year. That is not enough to cover the income tax bill of $31,804 in our example.

The point on concentrating on income tax expenses in retirement is that just looking at how much you have saved in tax deferred accounts is being short sighted. The amount of money in tax deferred accounts is not all yours. Uncle Sam is watching those accounts very carefully because he knows part of it belongs to him and he has no intention of not collecting from you.

How to Address the Retirement Tax Issue

The solution to lowering your tax bracket in retirement is not necessarily avoiding 401(k)s and IRAs in the saving years of life. That would be the wrong approach. For example, many companies that provide 401(k) plans offer a match. The match is FREE MONEY. Never turn down legitimate free money. As I suggested in Chapter 7, always, contribute to a 401(k) plan up to the matching amount and then the next $5,500 for those younger than 50, should be invested using a Roth IRA. Contributions to Roth IRAs are not tax deductible. The funds grow tax deferred and if the account has been open for at least five years, any funds withdrawn after the owner turns 59½, avoids all income taxes under present laws. The other advantage of a Roth IRA is there is no requirement to take a required minimum distribution at age 70½.

It is difficult to contribute a lot of money into a Roth because of IRS rules. I mentioned the $5,500 limit for those under 50. The limit for those over 50 is $6,500 per year. There is also an annual income limit that forbids higher income earners from contributing to a Roth. There is a way around this limitation.[4]

In his book, *The Power of Zero: How to Get to the 0% Tax Bracket and Transform Your Retirement*[5], David McKnight demonstrates ways to get to much lower tax brackets, if not zero, in retirement. It takes planning and the planning should start 10 to 15 years prior to retirement. Having money in IRAs and 401(k)s is not a deal breaker, but if you wish to minimize taxes in retirement, planning is essential.

Cash Value Life Insurance in Retirement

When many people think of life insurance, they focus on the fact that a life insurance policy provides money for their loved ones when the insured dies. That is its prime purpose, most of the time. However, cash value life insurance has tax advantages like a Roth IRA, but without the Roth IRA contribution limits. If you focus on the return of a cash value life policy versus that of a globally diversified equity portfolio, you are comparing apples and oranges. But if your focus is on lowering taxes in retirement, cash value life insurance should be a serious consideration.

Ed Slott, writing in the March 2016 issue of *National Underwriter Life & Health*[6], makes the argument for cash value life insurance in retirement. Slott is a practicing CPA located in Rockville Center, New York, and is recognized as an IRA expert. If I were to guess, it would be that Ed has made most of his money in the last few decades filling one-, two-, and three-day seminars dealing with the intricacies of IRAs. He is the author of more than a dozen books on

---

4 http://www.rothira.com/what-is-a-backdoor-roth-ira

5 The Power of Zero: How to Get to the 0% Tax Bracket and Transform Your Retirement, Acanthus Publishing Boston Massachusetts, 2013

6 www.LifeHealthPro.com, March 2016

the subject of IRAs and retirement. Slott states that he does not sell life insurance.[7]

In his March 2016 article, entitled *5 Best Arguments for Life Insurance,* Slott, lists the five reasons for the need for cash value life insurance in retirement.[8]

1. IRAs are a bad asset while life insurance is a good asset. He points to the fact that distributions from an IRA creates a tax event while distributions from a cash value life policy do not, if done correctly.[9]
2. He looks at cash value life policies as an investment, not an expense. He points out that once funds are disbursed from an IRA or 401(k), they are removed from not only tax risk, but the funds can be removed from stock market risk, with the right kind of policy.[10]
3. People think of life insurance in relation to a death benefit, but in many cases, people are not aware of the fact that life insurance can double as a retirement savings account.[11]
4. Distributions from a life policy are not subject to the required minimum distributions at age 70½ as are IRAs and 401(k)s. With IRAs and 401(k)s, even if you don't need income, once you reach 70½, you must take a distribution. Not so with cash value life insurance policy.[12]
5. Life insurance creates more life time wealth than any other investment because of leverage. Not only are distributions from a cash value life policy tax free, so is the death benefit providing heirs with tax free money in case of an early death.[13]

---

8 ibid

9 ibid

10 ibid

11 ibid

12 ibid

13 ibid

One aspect to cash value life insurance that Slott did not mention in the article is the availability of tax free funds during a down market. The worse time to take money from an investment account is when the market is down.

Consider a couple in retirement with all their savings in taxable accounts invested in a conservative 60/40 allocation; 60% equity and 40% fixed. In January they budget to take $100,000 out of their two million dollar IRA in December. When December rolls around, their account is down 15%. The $2,000,000 IRA is down to $1,700, 000. Taking another $100,000 will take it down to $1,600,000, which is lower by 25% from January. The scenario would be even worse if the budget was for $100,000 AFTER TAXES.

If they had a cash value life policy, the $100,000 could be taken from it and without tax consequences. If they were in a 20% tax bracket (for fed & state) and the $100,000 was before tax, they would only need $80,000 from the life policy.

The Case for Reverse Mortgages

Reverse mortgages have gotten a bad name over the years and rightly so. Some "advisors" pitched them as a way to free up equity in a home to use the money to buy an annuity. The "advisor" would pick up a hefty commission on the transaction and the home owner was often not well served. In addition, the cost of the reverse mortgage was expensive; sometimes more than the cost of selling a residence.

That all changed in 2011 and today costs can be on par with a traditional home mortgage. The Reverse Mortgage Stabilization Act of 2013 was passed, which put a limit on the amount of money that a reverse mortgage owner can receive in the first year of the contract. Immediately buying an annuity was no longer a way for "advisors," who did not have the best interest of the client in mind, from scoring a big commission. The Act also added protection for spouses who are too young to qualify (younger than 62), so they could stay in the home if the older spouse died.

Here is the way reverse mortgages work. At least one borrower (house owner) must be at least 62 years of age. The home must be owned or some or all the proceeds from a reverse mortgage must be used to pay off the mortgage, if a mortgage exists. Based on the age of the younger homeowner, the owners can gain access to about half of the appraised value of the home up to $625,500. Even if a home is appraised at $750,000, the loan amount will be based on $625,500. An older home owner qualifying for a lower interest rate qualifies for a higher loan amount; but not to exceed a maximum amount.

Those who qualify for a reverse mortgage can access the money in one of the following ways:

1. A line of credit
2. A monthly income stream
3. A cash loan

These are nonrecourse loans, meaning the issuer can seize the home but cannot seek out the home owner or their heirs for any further compensation, even if the home loses value over time. As long as one of the home owners' lives in the home and continues to pay real estate taxes, home owners insurance, and attends to regular maintenance, there is no payment due on the reverse mortgage.

Why use a reverse mortgage if you do not foresee a need for more money in retirement? There are a number of reasons. Here are a few:

The Investment Road We Travel

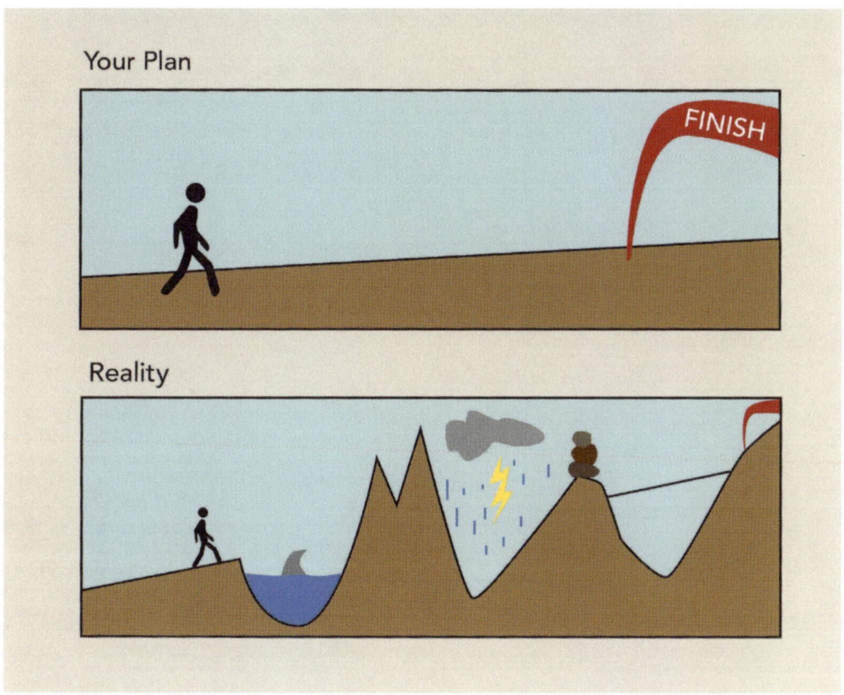

First, all plans must be reviewed and possibly adjusted because plans are a snapshot of where you are at a point in time and how to get you from that point to a place sometime in the future. On paper it is a smooth journey, but in real life it is like the graphic above. Everything changes, so having access to cash even if you never use it, can provide peace of mind.

Second, the funds made available from a reverse mortgage, represent tax free money. When you borrow money, the cash made available is a nontaxable event. The reverse mortgage loan does not have to be paid off until the last person leaves the home. The home is then sold to repay the loan amount plus any interest on money used during the term of the reverse mortgage. If the sale of the house exceeds the amount of the loan payoff, those funds go to the heirs or to the surviving home owner(s), if that is the case. If the sale of the house falls short of the loan payoff, the mortgage holder eats the loss.

Third, remember the availability of cash from life insurance to pay for tax free income for years when the market is down? A line of credit from a reverse mortgage affords the same benefit.

Finally, that same line of credit can be used in place of long term care insurance if the need arises. The longer you live, the greater the probability that you or your spouse will need long term care.

The End Game

Although taxes can be the biggest issue early in retirement, the cost of health care will sometimes become a bigger issue later on. As we age, the body needs more help from the medical profession. Medical costs increase as people age. There comes a time when many cannot function by themselves. In an article by Russ Banham and promoted by Lincoln Life, he states "Anyone reaching the age of 65 has a 40% chance of entering a nursing home, with a 20% chance of staying there for at least five years."[14]

Cost of care can differ depending on the type of care and the area of the country. Here is a chart from Genworth.[15]

14 http://online.wsj.com/ad/article/longtermcare-future

15 https://www.genworth.com/about-us/industry-expertise/cost-of-care.html

Health Care Costs Are Expensive

HOME HEALTH CARE

Homemaker Services[2]

Annual Cost	5-yr Annual Growth[3]
$45,760	2%

Home Health Aide[2]

Annual Cost	5-yr Annual Growth[3]
$46,332	1%

ADULT DAY HEALTH CARE[1]

Annual Cost
$17,680

5-yr Annual Growth[3]
3%

NURSING HOME CARE

Semi-Private Room[3]

Annual Cost	5-yr Annual Growth[3]
$82,125	3%

Private Room[5]

Annual Cost	5-yr Annual Growth[3]
$92,378	4%

ASSISTED LIVING FACILITY[4]

Annual Cost
$43,539

5-yr Annual Growth[3]
2%

© Genworth used with permission

Explanation of superscripts in "Cost of Medical Care is Expensive" graphic:
Genworth 2016 Cost of Care Survey conducted by Care Scout® April 2016

1 Based on 5 days per week by 52 weeks
2 Based on 44 hours per week by 52 weeks
3 Represents the compound annual growth rate based on Genworth Cost of Care Survey
4 Based on 12 months of care, private one bedroom
5 Based on 365 days of care

The cost of individual Long Term Care Insurance is expensive and the older you are when you apply for coverage, the higher the annual premium. Furthermore, if you never need care, paying two premiums each year, one for each spouse, for 20 to 30 years, means that you end up paying a lot of money for peace of mind.

There also are other ways to cover the possible need for long-term care.

There are life insurance companies that combine in one policy, both a death benefit and a long-term care rider, which can be used if necessary. They fit in very nicely with the use of life policies as sources of tax free cash in retirement.

Focus

I used to believe that planning for retirement meant socking away as much money as possible in 401(k) type plans and IRAs and that the retirement years would take care of themselves. Oh, it is true that I recognized the need for a way to cover Long Term Care and I knew the different stages of life that would happen in a 25 to 30 year retirement. Most of my clients were in their 30s, 40s and 50s. Now that I am working with many clients in retirement and planning for my own retirement, I realize that EVERY YEAR you must review how and from which accounts you will withdraw your retirement funds. If you don't, TAXES will eat up your hard earned savings. Further, I strongly advise, that starting no later than age 55, you begin planning how to move money out of 401(k) type plans and IRAs to investments that are more tax efficient.

CHAPTER 11

Withdrawal Rules in Retirement Are Different from Accumulation Rules

"The young man knows the rules, but the old man knows the exceptions."
- Oliver Wendell Holmes, Sr.

The conventional wisdom on the order in which you drawdown your funds in retirement are as follows:

1. Taxable Accounts, e.g. CDs, Non Retirement Brokerage Accounts
2. Tax Deferred Accounts e.g. IRAs, 401(k)s
3. Tax Free Accounts e.g. Roth IRAs, Cash Value Life Insurance
4. Non-Qualified Tax Deferred Accounts e.g. Annuities

The problem is that the conventional wisdom may not be wisdom at all. It does not take into account two major considerations. First, it may not be the way to make your retirement portfolio last the longest period of time. Second, and perhaps more importantly, it may not be the most tax efficient formula

As pointed out in Chapter 10, taxes in retirement can be a major expense. Plus, there are tax traps that can cause you expenses that are not immediately evident. Remember in Chapter 8, I said we would come back to Medicare costs and the importance of planning Each Year from where you are going to draw your income? Well here we go. The following is a primer on how Medicare is structured.

Medicare consists of the following parts:

Medicare Consists of the Following Parts:		
Part A	Free except for an annual deductible	Covers hospital stays, skilled care & Hospice
Part B	Monthly charge dependent on income	Covers doctors & outpatient visits
Part C	Monthly or annual charge	Covers charges not covered by Part B. Also known as Medicare Advantage. Usuallly also covers Part D
Part D	Co-pays & deductibles	Covers prescription drugs

Medicare Part C is usually available only in larger metropolitan areas. For those areas where Part C is not available, participants purchase what is known as a Medicare Supplement. They are available even in areas where Part C plans are available and therefore complete against Medicare Advantage plans. Medicare Supplements are sold by private insurance companies to cover those expenses not covered by Medicare Part B.

The premiums for Medicare Parts B and D are based on your modified adjusted gross income (MAGI) TWO YEARS PRIOR to the year you collect Medicare. Here is the table for Part B premiums in 2016;

The Premiums for Medicare Parts B & D are Based on your Modified Adjusted Gross Income

IF MODIFIED AGI FOR 2014 WAS & YOU FILE SINGLE	IF MARRIED AGI FOR 2014 WAS & MARRIED FILING JOINT	YOUR 2016 ANNUAL PREMIUM FOR PART B WILL BE*
$0 to $85,000	$0 to $170,000	$1,258.80 or $1,461.80
$85,001->$107,000	$170,001 -$214,000	$2,046.00
$107,001->$160,000	$214,001->$320,000	$2,923.20
$160,001->$214,000	$320,001->428,000	$3,800.40
Greater than $214,000	Greater than $428,000	$4,688.60

*The reason there are two figures for those in the first row showing dollar amounts, is because of a clause in the Social Security law that says if there is not a Cost of Living Adjustment (COLA) for a particular year, there cannot be a premium increase in the following year. In 2016, there was no COLA, therefore there was not an increase in Part B in 2016 for those who had collected benefits in 2015. They were said "To be Held Harmless" and paid a premium of $1,258.80. Those who first collected Medicare benefits in 2016 were subjected to the higher premium of $1,461.80.

Carefully consider the differences in the cost of premiums as the Modified AGI increases. The difference between $1,258.80 in tier one and $2,046 in tier two is $787.20. For a married couple, both of whom are collecting Medicare benefits, the total costs are twice that amount: $1,574.40.

Medicare Part D premiums are also affected by Modified AGI. Here is the table for Part D premiums in 2016;

Modified Adjusted Gross Income Can Cause Higher Medicare Premiums

MAGI	PART B MONTHLY PREMIUM	PRESCRIPTION DRUG MONTHLY PREMIUM
INDIVIDUALS: $85,000 or less MFJ: $170,000 or less	2015 Standard Premium = $121.80	Your Plan Premium
INDIVIDUALS: $85,001 to $107,000 MFJ: $170,001 to $214,000	Standard Premium + $48.70	Your Plan Premium + $12.70
INDIVIDUALS: $107,001 to $160,000 MFJ: $214,001 to $320,000	Standard Premium + $121.80	Your Plan Premium + $32.80
INDIVIDUALS: $160,001 to $214,000 MFJ: $320,001 to $428,000	Standard Premium + $194.90	Your Plan Premium + $52.80
INDIVIDUALS: Above $214,000 MFJ: Above $428,000	Standard Premium + 268.00	Your Plan Premium + $72.90

MFJ: Married Filing Joint

With what you learned in Chapter 10 about taxes in your retirement years and now this increase in premium Medicare costs looming for you two years down the road, it should be clear by now that planning your income sources EACH YEAR is of paramount importance. Increased taxable income not only means higher federal and state taxes, it also means higher premiums for Medicare Parts B & D. The bottom line: Fewer spendable dollars for you and your spouse!

For example, if you cross a particular Modified Adjusted Gross Income[1] (MAGI) amount in one tax year, you could see your Medicare costs rise in a subsequent year. The Social Security Administration uses your latest tax information received from the IRS to review costs for parts B and D of Medicare.[2] For example, an increase in Medicare costs in 2018 would most likely be based on your 2016 income tax return.

The Dreaded Age 70½

You may recall that on January 1, 2011, the first set of baby boomers turned 65 and therefore became eligible for Medicare. Big headlines about 10,000 boomers turning 65 every day for the next 19 years were all over the press.

The headlines were not as big about those same boomers turning 70½ starting July 1, 2016. Strange that most of the articles I read about the July 1, 2016, date, still quote the same number, i.e. 10,000, turning 70½ five years later. Either the number was wrong in 2011 or it is wrong in 2016, but it doesn't matter. It is a big number and Uncle Sam is smiling while wearing tax collector's hat.

Natalie Choate is an attorney who is recognized as an expert in the areas of estate planning and retirement benefits. Her book, **Life & Death Planning for Retirement Benefits**[3] is in its seventh edition (AtaxPlan Publications Boston, MA).

---

1 MAGI =Adjusted Gross Income (bottom line on page 1 of Form 1040 plus certain deductions taken that must be added back. Examples of deductions that must be added back in are one half of self-employment tax and Passive loss or passive gains.

2 Social Security Administration Publication #05-10536

3 AtaxPlan Publications Boston MA

In a video on the InvestementNewsVideos website[4], Ms. Choate talks about a way to meet your Required Minimum Distribution (RMD) without having it add to your Adjusted Gross Income. For clients who have a charitable intent, they can have the distribution paid directly to the charity of their choice. By doing so, the RMD is satisfied and your Adjusted Gross income is not affected. Adjusted Gross Income affects Medicare premiums, medical expenses, taxability of Social Security benefits, the phase-out of personal deductions and the sur tax on investment income. This method of satisfying your RMD works for all income tax payers but can be particularly helpful for lower income retirees. You must make sure that the distribution is paid directly to the charity and you have reached age 70½, if you use this section of the IRS code.

Natalie Choate was born in 1945 and said she was turning 70½ in 2016 according to an article in the Wall Street Journal[5]. She was interviewed by Laura Saunders of *The Wall Street Journal* during which Natalie was quoted as saying "Now I have sympathy for average people facing these decisions,"[6] referring to RMDs. A more revealing comment she made during the interview was that she followed her own advice and saved to the max and now finds her withdrawals are more complex than expected. She has nine IRAs that total more than $1 million dollars.

Here is what the Internal Revenue Service code states about taking the first RMD. The first Required Minimum Distribution must be

---

4 https://www.bing.com/videos/search?q=investment+news+video+Natalie+Choate &&view=detail&mid=CD00EE14FF148F5F0F0BCD00EE14FF148F5F0F0B&FORM =VRDGAR

5 http://www.wsj.com/articles/when-the-ira-expert-reaches-withdrawal-age-1464341400

made by April 1 of the year following the year when you turn 70½[6]. (If that sounds confusing, you must remember, there are very few areas that the federal government touches that are easily understood.) Since Ms. Choate turned 70½ in 2016, she can wait until April 1, 2017, to take her 2016 RMD. Here is what happens if she takes that distribution in January, February, or March of 2017.

Let's say her Traditional IRAs were worth a total of $1,250,000 on December 31, 2015. Her RMD for 2016 will be $45,620. If she does not take a distribution in 2016, but waits until the first three months of 2017, she has to take a second distribution in 2017 to satisfy the 2017 RMD. If the account was worth about the same amount on December 31, 2016, as it was the year before, her two deductions in 2017 amount to withdrawals of over $90,000 in the taxable year of 2017. She may want to send all of that directly to a charity, but I doubt it.

Natalie Choate's story is revealing because it emphasizes the major point of this chapter. It is one thing to know how to save for retirement. It is quite another to know how to structure your savings so that the trap set by the Internal Revenue Service for you does not ruin your retirement. I am not referring to the trap of using the April 1st date of year following your 70½ birthday. I am referring to having all of your retirement funds in tax deferred accounts like IRAs, 401(k)s and 403(b)s.

Solving for Income Strategies

As I mentioned in chapter 10, beginning no later than age 55, you should start to plan how you will move funds out of qualified

6 Internal Revenue Service Publication 560

accounts, (i.e. accounts that are growing tax deferred and therefore subject to tax when you withdraw those funds), to accounts that will provide tax-free income so that you can minimize taxes in retirement. So the questions is; "Where should you move them?" Here are a couple of options.

Use Roth IRAs

We talked about moving funds from traditional IRAs to Roth IRAs. This should be part of your plan each year. Open a Roth as early as possible. A Roth IRA can be opened for as little as $100. For Roth's to avoid the 10% penalties on withdrawals, the Roth must be in existence for at least five years and the owner must be at least 59½ to avoid any taxes. One exception to the 10% penalty is that you can withdraw any after-tax contribution and not be subject to the 10% penalty.

The clock for having the Roth opened for 5 years is based on the year the account is opened and funded. The clock does not start again each time money is added to the account.

Use of Section 72t of the Code

Section 72t of the Internal Revenue Code allows withdrawals from a traditional IRA while avoiding the 10% penalty. If you are younger than 59½, you can withdraw funds from a traditional IRA using 72t and avoid the 10% penalty subject to the following rules:

1. The funds must be withdrawn in substantially equal amounts over a minimum of five years or until the owner reaches the age of 59½, whichever is longer.
2. Once the process is started, it is extremely difficult to change it.

For example, at age 50, you could start withdrawing funds in substantially equal amounts each year for 10½ years and not be subject to the 10% penalty. The withdrawals would be taxable but you avoided the penalty.

Here's another example; a person age 55 could use Section 72t to start withdrawing funds in substantially equal amounts for five years and avoid the 10% penalty.

When do you use Section 72t? If you have built up a substantial amount in a traditional IRA, you could use the annual incomes made available by using 72t to purchase a cash value life policy. That would move funds from a taxable account to a fund that would afford tax free money in retirement, which could be used for either health care issues or for living expenses in retirement years when the stock market is down.

401(k)s & Exceptions to the 10% Penalty

A person, who participates in an employer 401(k) plan, who leaves employment at age 55 or older, can withdraw funds from the plan without having the funds subject to the 10% penalty. It is in the code. I used the exception myself.

I am not in favor of borrowing from a 401(k) plan, but taking out a loan from a 401(k) to pay for a cash value life policy might make sense if the 401(k) has built up a substantial amount of value. Loans from a 401(k) usually must be repaid within five years. If not repaid within the five year period, it's considered a disbursement, subject to taxes and the 10% penalty, if the owner is younger than 59½.

Focus

There are three types of workers who will start planning for their Golden Years when they reach about age 55.

1. The folks in the first group will wake up to the fact that in the next decade or so, they will be retired and they have no idea where the money they will live off will come from. Social Security by itself will not cut it.
2. The second group will continue to pour as much money as they can, into tax deferred accounts, thinking that one to two million dollars will create a comfortable life style after leaving the work force. It will not dawn on them until it is too late that the Internal Revenue Service is anxiously waiting for their cut of that one to two million.
3. The third group will start planning to move the money out of their tax deferred accounts so that their Golden Years will indeed be Golden.

Make sure you are in Group 3!

CONCLUSIONS

If you have reached this page because you have read all eleven chapters, I thank you and hope you gained at least a few ideas, either about how to invest using an academic approach or about how to plan more carefully so that you do not carry a big tax burden throughout your years in retirement.

If you are concentrating on climbing the mountain, that is, the accumulation phase, understand that all investing involves risk. Stock picking, marketing timing and track record investing will cause you grief. Trying to get rich quickly will be to your detriment. Every stock, bond, mutual fund and ETF has a prospectus that states some variation of "Past performance is not a guarantee of future results." It is probably the most ignored piece of advice in the investment world or closely tied with "This time it's different." The climb up the mountain is not a paved trail. It is not a gentle slope. There will be times when the path will take you down for a while before it starts back up. Educate yourself and ask lots of questions. After all, it is your money and you deserve a comfortable and peaceful retirement.

If you are concentrating on getting safely down the mountain, that is, the distribution phase, make sure you plan how you are going to limit your tax burden before the start of each new year. The ideas and examples I have given you are not to be taken as tax advice. They are ideas and examples to take to your CPA or whoever you use to prepare your taxes. You want to find a professional who knows the tax code and provides legal, moral and ethical advice. The first three and a half months of next year, is not the time to prepare for the year just ended. The time to plan for those already in retirement is May through November. For those of you who are within ten to fifteen years of retirement, the time is NOW. Some of the examples I have suggested take years to implement. Wait too long and they will be lost to you.

I wish you success and safety, regardless of where you are on the mountain.

W.T. Mullen
October 1, 2016

RECOGNITIONS

An author can never act alone and achieve success in getting a book published. I have been helped by some of the best, both in getting the final product looking respectable and keeping me focused on assuring that the information is in a readable and understandable format.

Stacy Dymalski has been a tremendous source of information. Her book, "**Nine Steps to Self-Publishing Your Book**" has been a great help but her personal attention to detail in providing feedback has been invaluable. Before I began writing the manuscript I thought I was fairly attentive to grammar but Stacy's proof reading has me reevaluating that thought.

Thanks to Michelle Rayner for an exceptional job in creating the cover and her work on the graphics and charts in the book. Her creativity has added much to the book.

Katie Mullaly took all that was put to paper and organized it in a readable and understandable flow.

Finally, thank you Carole Mullen, my wife, for all the times you have read the manuscript after every change and update. She spent part of the day on the 29th anniversary of our wedding reading edition number eleven.

ABOUT THE AUTHOR

Bill Mullen is the managing member of Mullennium Finance LLC, a Utah Registered Investment Advisory firm. Bill's focus is fee-only investment advising, matching portfolios that mirror a client's risk tolerance and timeline. Bill helps guide professionals and retirees toward achieving and maintaining lifelong financial independence. Mullennium Finance is unique in that they are one of the very few local firms that teach free market investment strategy. Every client is first coached, and then provided with a detailed strategy based on their stated goals, risk tolerance and objectives. We live in a world of financial chaos: market volatility, information overload, and unlimited financial products from which to choose. Bill and his team at Mullennium Finance help break down that chaos into an easy to understand and carefully managed framework.

For more information about Bill and Mullennium Finance visit http://savinginvestors.com/.

A HANDY REMINDER

Everyone needs a reminder, so cut this out and keep it on your fridge to remind yourself that a successful retirement demands lots of planning.

How to Diffuse Your Ticking Tax Time Bomb

SAVE FIRST, SPEND WHAT IS LEFT OVER

OWN EQUITIES, DIVERSIFY GLOBALLY, REBALANCE

PREPARE FOR RETIREMENT BY MOVING OUT OF TAXABLE ACCOUNTS

WORK WITH A TAX PLANNER WHO IS A FIDUCIARY

If you get stuck on anything, contact me, Bill Mullen at bill@billmullen.org.

END NOTES

The information in this communication should not be construed as investment, tax or legal advice and may not be relied on for the purpose of avoiding any Federal tax penalty. All information is believed to be from reliable sources; however we make no representation as to its completeness or accuracy. All economic and performance data is historical and not indicative of future results. Market indices discussed are unmanaged. Investors cannot invest in unmanaged indices. The publisher is not engaged in rendering legal, accounting or other professional services. If assistance is needed, the reader is advised to engage the services of a competent professional. This material was prepared by Bill Mullen. Bill has been a Certified Financial Planner Practitioner™ for 24 years and is the Managing Member of Mullennium Finance LLC, a Fee Only Utah Licensed Investment Advisor. Bill works with individuals and small business owners to diversify their portfolios and reduce their taxes. Mullennium Finance LLC is located in Park City, Midway, Heber City and Salt Lake City in Utah. All investing involve risk. Always read the prospectus before investing. Past performance is no guarantee of future performance.

IRS CIRCULAR 230 NOTICE: In order to comply with certain IRS regulations regarding tax advice, we inform you that unless expressly stated otherwise, any tax advice contained in this communication (including any attachments) is not intended or written to be used, and cannot be used, for purposes of (i) avoiding penalties under the Internal Revenue Code or (ii) promoting, marketing or recommending to another party any transaction or matter addressed here.